D0866867

ENGLISH LITERATURE
AND THE CLASSICS

ENGLISH LITERATURE AND THE CLASSICS

Tragedy by GILBERT MURRAY
Platonism by J. A. STEWART
Theophrastus by G. S. GORDON
Greek Romances by J. S. PHILLIMORE
Ciceronianism by A. C. CLARK
Vergil by H. W. GARROD
Ovid by S. G. OWEN
Satura by R. J. E. TIDDY
Senecan Tragedy by A. D. GODLEY

Collected by G. S. GORDON

NEW YORK / RUSSELL & RUSSELL

FIRST PUBLISHED IN 1912
REISSUED, 1969, BY RUSSELL & RUSSELL
A DIVISION OF ATHENEUM PUBLISHERS, INC.
L. C. CATALOG CARD NO: 68-15126
PRINTED IN THE UNITED STATES OF AMERICA

PREFACE

THIS book is a collection of nine lectures delivered in Oxford at the invitation of the Board of English Studies in the winter of 1911–12. They were addressed primarily to members of the English School, but in effect to all students of modern literature in the University who cared to hear, from students of ancient literature, something of what the Classics mean in the history of letters. The story of the Ancients and Moderns is a story, happily, without conclusion, which has its sequel and its public in every generation. These lectures, here and there expanded, but printed, for the most part, as they were given, are now offered as an instalment of that story to the larger circle of readers.

G. S. G.

OXFORD,
September, 1912.

CONTENTS

GREEK AND ENGLISH TRAGEDY

A CONTRAST

By Gilbert Murray

The right way to meet a great work of art is not to come with fixed expectations and demands of your own, but simply to listen and allow it to speak. And I believe that any sensitive person who comes to a Greek play with his imagination fairly alert and his mind ready to accept what is given him, will generally feel keen enjoyment in both the drama and the poetry. But the trouble is that we cannot rid ourselves of our preconceptions. We come full of expectation that it will be like Shakespeare or like Racine, or like church, or like some private *a priori* notion of what a Greek play ought to be, and when it proves different we are disappointed and spend our time in searching for something that is not there, and not observing what is.

I wish in this lecture merely to discuss the first fundamental contrast [1] between Greek and English tragedy, that the English tragedy is primarily an entertainment, the Greek a religious ritual. True, the entertainment has gradually become ennobled:

---

[1] For some other sides of the question I may refer to my essay on 'What English Poetry may still learn from Greek', published this year (1912) in *Essays and Studies by Members of the English Association*, Vol. III.

its 'true intent' is for something higher than the mere 'delight' of the audience; and the religious ritual has been transformed by many influences, chiefly by the simple fact that it was conducted by born artists and watched by sensitive spectators, till it became also an artistic entertainment.   But something of the origin remains.

I will take for granted a certain archaeological account of the birth and nature of Greek tragedy. Its details will be questioned by many scholars, but its broad outline admitted by almost all; and it is only the broad outline that matters for our present purpose.   Fundamentally Tragedy was the mimetic dance of the Dionysus Religion developed and transfigured by certain influences that we shall consider later.   It was a ritual dance, a *Drômenon*, or 'Thing Done', a *Sacer Ludus*; under slightly different circumstances it would have been a mystery.

It was a dance; not of course a dance like our dances, a mere gay movement of the feet.   A primitive dance was the use of the whole body, the whole being, to express that overflow of dim thought or emotion which could not express itself in articulate speech.   The dance is a rhythmical yearning of the whole body towards the emotion that we cannot define, the desire that is beyond our power to compass.

And it was the dance of the Dionysus Religion. What was that Religion ?   Let us not confuse the issue by asking 'Who was Dionysus ?'   To that question there is no answer, because of course there was no such person.   Dionysus was a fiction, the ritual of Dionysus a reality—the reality in fact out of which the fiction was developed or projected. It is the ritual of the Spring, of the New Year, of ' le Renouveau '—the Renewal after the dead winter of all the life of the world. Such rituals regularly generate out of themselves shadowy daimones or spirits or gods. This vegetation ritual is so widespread that the so-called ' vegetation-spirit '—the personified life of the world which fades, dies, and is reborn : the 'he' that we call 'it' when we say that 'it' is raining or fine or cold—has many different names and constitutes an element in innumerable worships. I have tried elsewhere to show how deeply the external form of Tragedy has been affected by the ritual of this worship and the recurrent life-history of this Year-spirit, who meets his enemy, dies, and is announced as dead, is wept for, rediscovered, and revived in glory.[1]

Tragedy, then, is the dance of this religion of the Renouveau, developing under three main influences. First, like all Greek literature and art, it fell under the sway of the Epic, both the poems that we call ' Homer ' and the lost poems that were so called in the sixth century B. C., an influence rich in legendary and romantic material, secular, aristocratic, and, as Eratosthenes observed, written for entertainment. Tragedy extended its subject-matter, beyond Dionysus or any mere Renouveau-spirit, first to other vegetation-heroes of divers sorts, then to all the heroes of Epic. A second influence came from the great figures or events of recent or contemporary

---

[1] In *Themis* by J. E. Harrison, pp. 341–63. See in general Frazer's *Attis Adonis Osiris*.

history, provided only that they were sufficiently in-
spiring or 'tragic'. We must remember that there
was then no distinction between history and myth :
the death of Agamemnon was as much history as the
defeat of Xerxes. But of course contemporary history seemed as a rule comparatively near to prose
and unheroic ; it needed tremendous events like the
sack of Miletus or the repulse of Persia, or great
permanent issues like the struggle against tyrants, to
win their way into tragedy. Most of all tragedy was
influenced, like other forms of art, by its own inherent
nature. When you have once begun to act, and to
act great themes of life and death, you cannot, if you
are an artist, help moving in a particular direction.
You are in the world of drama, and things that are
dramatic will seize you and carry you along. Greek
tragedy as we know it is drama, and intense drama.
That indeed is obvious. The thing that we have
to realize is that through it all there remains the
spirit of the *Sacer Ludus*. It is drama, but it is
also religion.

But, you will say, is this not playing with words ?
In what sense does this dance of Dionysus deserve
the name of religion at all ? It is a point that we
must exert our imaginations a little to understand.
We think of religion as something moralized; we
have even had it defined, inadequately enough, as
'morality touched with emotion'. Now this religion
of the Renouveau is not, in our sense of the word,
much moralized, but it has at least this of religion
about it : that it is always concerned with our rela-

tion to great world-forces. It brings human life into contact with something tremendous that is outside human life; it is a striving towards some sort of harmony of man with his whole unseen environment; it aims at that great prize, or great illusion, the being at peace with God. Further, if we would understand Dionysus-worship, we must realize that these vegetation-cults amid all their grossness were bound up with the things that are most beautiful in the world. It is true that there is little description of scenery in the literature of the ancient Greeks. They did not describe forests and mountains; they worshipped them and built temples in them. Their love for nature was that of the mountaineer or the seaman, who does not talk much about sea or mountain, but sickens and pines if he is taken away from them. And even the literature, if free from actual descriptions of scenery, is full of flowers and garlands, and shot through by the light of the stars and the moon—things that we have superseded and seldom even see, but that were familiar if half-divine companions to every Greek.

This religion had the element of beauty; it had also that of mystery. It was born of primitive wonder and desire, and it moved in a region which is still perhaps the most mysterious of all that are forced upon our daily attention, the region of growth and of renewed life. It had, lastly, what we are apt to forget, the element of peril, peril common to the whole community and ever recurrent. Even in the eighteenth century the ancient feeling about this might have been understood. Now, when the agriculture of the world is open and trade international, we have almost ceased to notice the harvests of the year in any particular place. But in early Greece every little community depended on the produce of its own small plot of land ; its agriculture was timid and helpless ; it had hungry and more or less hostile neighbours on every side ; the autumn store of food was usually eaten before the next harvest. The poet Alcman, describing the seasons, mentions spring as the time ' when the world is budding but there is not enough to eat '. [1] It is worth remembering, too, that primitive men draw no very clear line of demarcation between themselves and their animals and even vegetables, and Greek is full of words which can apply to all three, ἔρνος, θάλος, φίτυμα, and the like : the thing that is common to them is that they are all young and all children of Earth the Mother. Every autumn these men would see the crops cut, the fields bare and hard, the trees without leaves, a dead world everywhere round them, and the year's stock of food beginning to dwindle inevitably away. Every winter one thought would be in all minds, the longing that the spirit, whoever he was, Dionysus, Osiris, Adonis, would be duly reborn and bring *Sotêria*—Deliverance, the dread that he might fail to return and the world remain dead. And probably every few years, if we knew the unwritten history of these centuries, we should find that for some little community the dead god did not rise again, and they would wait wondering, full of the sense of horrible and unpardoned sin, despairing or performing ghastly rites, waiting till

[1] Alcman, fr. 76 (B⁴).

famine finished them off, or their neighbours discovered that they were weak enough to be safely
enslaved.

We must not forget, too, the personality, definite
and almost human, of this Rebirth in the mind of
primitive man. Primitive man needed so very little
to create a person from; he needed no human shape,
indeed no shape at all: that thing, whatever it was,
that was in the new trees and flowers or the new
vintage, that thing itself was a person—it might be
Dionysus; it might be the Korê or Maiden—and,
what is more, it was the same person who had been
here at the beginning of last year and then had died.
It was always a return, a rebirth. Just so the new
generation of tribesmen were the old ancestors
returned, safe from the keeping of Earth the ancient
Life-giver. They looked forward normally not to
some remote heaven, but to a cycle of life, death,
and return from death, a return on which everything
depended and for which the tribe prayed as their
salvation.

There is obviously religion in this, and it is a
religion that branches off into various other forms.
For instance, tragedy is full of the religion of the
Suppliant, the man or woman who is stricken down
by the world and has no help left but prayer. This
conception seems very probably to be somehow
associated with the suffering and dying god. At
any rate Greek tragedy is full of suppliant plays, or
plays which at least centre upon some altar of
refuge. There is perhaps no other single motive
so prominent; and it is worth realizing that often

when this power of the suppliant, this compulsion
upon the most high gods to avenge the wrongs
of the helpless, is not insisted upon, it is at least
passionately denied.   Tragedy is haunted by the
atmosphere ; for to cry bitterly that the sun will
not turn back in heaven

> For the wrongs of man, the cry
> Of his ailing tribes assembled,
> To do justice ere they die,[1]

is, as far as atmosphere goes, much the same thing
as to assert that he will.

And is the Year Ritual after all so non-moral?
It looks so at first sight to one who comes to it
with modern or Christian expectations.   Things
that seem to us gross and licentious are actually
among its prescribed rites.   Yet in reality it is
moralized through and through, moralized to excess.
The very things we complain of are proofs of this.
The natural world is conceived throughout as framed
on the same model as the human society, and
responding to the same motives as the tribe itself.
Consequently actions which in general tend to
stimulate human fecundity are ritually desirable as
increasing the fertility of the fields.   On the other
hand, offences against marriage laws and sexual
taboos are severely punished : they will bring blight
and famine.   It is the same with greater issues.
The whole process of nature was regarded as moral
and human.   When the summer was too hot or the
winter too cold, it was 'injustice' and sure to be

---

[1] Eur. *El.* 740 f.

punished. Every year the Sun himself regularly committed ' Hubris ', the sin of pride, and that pride was chastised by a proper fall. The early philosophers are full of this moralized physical science. ' The Sun shall not transgress his measures : if he does, he shall be pursued by Erinyes, ministers of Justice.' It is the law of all existing things : ' they all pay retribution for injustice one to another according to the ordinance of Time.'[1] The life-history of each Year-Daemon was an example of this refluent balance. Each in his turn came as an avenger— or, what amounts to the same, as the wronged one re-risen ; each slew the slayer, then waxed great in his pride and must in the end himself be slain. It was all as it should be, all as the eternal cycle had ordained. Conceptions like this are very clearly religious, and we all know their profound importance in Greek tragedy. They may almost be said to form the general ground-scheme on which each particular tragedy is built.

These considerations lead us straight to one great contrast. In all Greek tragedies, even those that are full of free thought, the whole permeating atmosphere is that of religion. What is it with us ? The answer is not difficult. Our stage demands beautiful women as actresses ; the shopwindows are filled with their portraits ; our lighter and more popular stage lives by its sexual appeal. The Greeks had no women on the stage and their men wore masks, masks that never had aimed at being

[1] Heraclitus, fr. 94 D ; Anaximander, fr. 9 D.

particularly beautiful, but were first magical, then sacred, and in the end at least a matter of dignified convention. The same lesson is taught by the almost invariable presence of a pair of lovers in all modern works of fiction. Our permeating atmosphere is that of love between the sexes. We are the descendants not of the tragedians but of the *scriptores erotici*. No doubt we have plays on the most varied subjects, plays of intrigue or adventure —subjects which are akin to romance and in which the love interest is generally strong—plays of war, of patriotism, of social reform. A few peculiar plays sometimes succeed in escaping altogether from the pervading atmosphere, but they only do so by a deliberate and anti-popular effort. Now of course the love motive occurs in Greek tragedy again and again : Euripides is predominantly interested in it ; so do the motives of intrigue, adventure, or war ; but observe in each case how it is coloured by religion. When we moderns introduce brave warriors we mostly think of them as winning or failing to win the love of fair ladies ; when Aeschylus speaks of war he speaks like this :— he tells how the city-sacking hosts of Persia

'have thrown a path, and nailed it with many nails for a yoke upon the neck of the sea.
The fierce lord of multitudinous Asia driveth the flock that god hath given him forth over all the world ; in his hard true captains he hath put his trust, the man like unto a god, of the seed of the shower of gold. His eyes shine dark with a bloody serpent's glare : with many hands and with many ships and the sweep of the chariots of Syria he

bringeth down upon brave spearmen the bowman's battle that quelleth from afar.

Who shall be trusted to stem the great stream of men? Who with strong bars to prison the swell of the uncontrollable sea? For none may come near to the army of Persia, and courage is in the heart of her people.

For a doom from God hath prevailed from long ago, and hath laid for a charge upon the Persians the wars that strike at towers and the noise and gladness of battling horsemen and the turning of cities in the dust. And they have learned, when the wide sea grows grey with the wrath of the wind, they have learned to look upon the holy places of the deep, trusting in their cables subtly-built and engines that carry nations.

Yet the deep thought and the guile of God, what mortal man can hide therefrom? Who is he of the nimble foot, who is master of such light leaping? For with love and false smiling at the first Ate brings him to the net, whence it is not for mortal man to climb over and flee away.'[1]

When our heroines die for love they do it in a personal and sentimental way, because their feelings are more than they can bear. When Phaedra dies for love it is in part a definite attempt to save her honour, in part almost a yielding of herself upon an altar.

> Let me be
> To sate the Cyprian who is murdering me!
> To-day shall be her day; and, all strife past,
> Her bitter love shall quell me at the last.

And the temptress who leads her into her troubles

[1] Aesch. *Persae* 73 ff. I accept Kirchhoff's order for the verses, suggested by O. Müller.

has spoken very little about Phaedra's feelings : she has dwelt on love not as a personal emotion but as a world-power.

A most strong Goddess hath swept down on thee...
She ranges with the stars of eve and morn ;
She wanders in the heaving of the sea ;
And all life lives from her.[1]

Similar passages might be cited by the score. The rule is that in Greek tragedy every great emotion is treated as an instance of a world-force : its background and atmosphere are made by Religion.

Of course there is development in all art. We start here with a sacred ritual and we end with an exciting drama. The most essential part of the ritual is the dance, the collective or communal dance of a band of worshippers, and this actually survives throughout the whole growth of tragedy. But here, too, there is development, from the first stage of pure magic, where thirsty tribesmen dance the rain-dance to fill the wells, not thinking at all about their appearance, only straining every nerve to get water, to the last stage in which the accomplished pro-fessional dancer simply comes forward to exhibit his or her gracefulness. Neither of these extreme stages is found in Greek tragedy ; tragedy moves some-where between the two ; and it is obviously somewhere between the two that the right artistic point lies. There is probably no extreme beauty in the first stage, except in fragments ; and the last is, I think, clearly condemned by the mere directness of its

[1] Eur. *Hippolytus* 447 ff., 725 ff.

attack. Any work of art which confessedly comes
before us saying, ' Just look at me ! See how beautiful
I am ! ' must in some measure fail of its effect. For
one thing, it utters a challenge and suggests a re-
pulsion ; for another, there seems to be almost a law
that beauty should always be a bye-product, the
mere result of doing a thing right or trying to express
something as well as you can. In Greek tragedy
one can see clearly the remains of the magic dances :
there is a chorus in Aeschylus' *Suppliants* where the
Danaids call upon the divine cow their ancestress
and imitate the way she cropped flowers in a meadow
(ll. 40 ff.) ; and the play ends with a lovely and almost
undisguised rain-dance. In the *Oedipus Rex* the first
chorus represents a magic dance, full of hoots and
shouts, for driving away pestilence. The chorus in
the *Medea*, on the other hand, has nothing magical
about it : its chief use is purely dramatic, to sympathize, to soften, to shed over the play its lyrical
splendour, and at one supreme moment to beat
vainly upon a barred door behind which a woman is
murdering her child.

Tragedy developed, as I have said, under various
influences. But most of all its own inherent instinct
led it steadily in the direction of drama. It ceased
merely to wail for a death and dance for a resurrec-
tion. It began to study character and human feeling :
to think what sort of person died and what sort of
person killed him, and why he did it, and how they
both felt and what things they may be supposed to
have said to express their feelings. It developed
the interest in character as character and in situation

as situation.   Now the psychology of a divine being is almost inevitably monotonous and uninteresting. Consequently the stories were humanized.   The old gods were made into human heroes.   When we think of Agamemnon and Oedipus, of Clytemnestra and Phaedra, it is hard to realize that they were ever mere gods or daimones.   Yet we know that they were.   It is the hand of the dramatist that has drawn them down from heaven and made them living and human and full of character.

But here comes a remarkable fact.   The instinct for drama is notoriously a dangerous guide.   It leads most stage-writers to look out for the effect, not the truth ; to write with a view to exciting or amusing the audience rather than expressing some real thing which they have to express.   It leads to staginess, to the stage hero and heroine, the stage villain, to stage psychology in general.   In Greek tragedy this kind of falseness is almost entirely absent.   It has no utter villains, no insipidly angelic heroines. Even its tyrants have some touch of human nature about them : they have at least a case to state. Even its virgin-martyrs are not waxen images.   The psychology is not the psychology of melodrama, specially contrived so as to lead to 'situations'.   It is that of real human nature imaginatively observed or profoundly felt.   Even if we leave Euripides out of account, what poet until quite modern times would have dared to make us sympathize with Clytemnestra, the bloodstained adulteress, as Aeschylus does ? Who would have dared, like Sophocles, to make Antigone speak cruelly to her devoted sister, or Electra, with all sympathies concentrated on her, behave like a wild beast and be disgusted at herself for so doing ?[1]

What makes this psychological sincerity the more striking is that it exists in the midst of such elaborate and severe convention, in such utter absence of realism. People sometimes suppose that a rigid convention implies insincerity, or, more absurd still, a slack and careless convention truthfulness. Consider George Meredith's sonnet-sequence, *Modern Love*; that is all written in a stiff sonnet-like convention, in verse, in rhymed verse, in verse that has to rhyme in a peculiar and elaborate manner. Yet the great quality of the poem is its subtle and sincere psychology. And take on the other side a sloppy melodramatic novel, in which the convention is as slack as can be, but the description of character may be quite false and 'conventional'. Convention in artistic form has nothing to do with conventionality of thought. The Greek poet when describing his heroine's state of mind may have to do so by putting into her lips a long formal speech on the subject, beginning—in the language of our translations—'In the first place on the one hand . . .' That is a convention of form. But what she says in that set speech will be not only beautiful in thought and language, but curiously truthful also, instinct both with sympathy and with ruthlessness.

Am I trying to make out that there is no falseness, no utterly improbable fiction, in Greek tragedy?

[1] Soph. *Electra* 616 ff.

Not at all. Most of the stories contain impossibilities. But I think you will find, if you compare the Greek drama with the modern, that while the false elements in modern plays are due to the amatory or romantic atmosphere and chiefly affect the character drawing, in Greek they are due to the religious and chiefly affect the background of the story. Almost all the recorded history of the past was, in the fifth century, a tissue of myth and fable. The heroic saga, the normal stuff of tragedy, was all more or less supernatural; and the Greeks accepted, and even enjoyed, the intrusion of frankly supernatural beings, of oracles and *hieroi logoi*. Clytemnestra was the daughter of Leda, bride of the divine Swan; her half-brothers were thoroughly miraculous demi-gods. Electra was betrothed in marriage to one of these demi-gods. Yet when you study the characters of Clytemnestra and Electra in all three tragedians you will find them both human and severely true.

Aristotle observes, in speaking of the gradual development of tragedy, that 'after passing through many changes it found its proper form and there stopped' (*Poet.* 49A 15). The words have a curious truth. Its 'proper form' was a very strange one, unlike that of any drama before or since. It never forgot its origin; it moved, as it were, in two planes, keeping always present, in the very heart of its action, the sacred Chorus of fifteen, shadowy persons, in part human creatures, in part incarnate shapes of meditation and emotion. It kept its gigantic masked figures, its long formal speeches, every speech be-

ginning at the beginning of a verse and ending at the
end of a verse. It kept its messengers, its prologues,
and its divine epiphanies. And inside this grandiose
shell it created a peculiar kind of beauty, a rhythm
of high yet intoxicating emotion, a religious and
poignant sincerity, which no other form of drama has
quite attained. At one period indeed it looked as
if tragedy was beginning to move away from its
stiffness. When Sophocles reminds modern critics
of Shakespeare it is in part because he began, very
cautiously and delicately, to do to tragedy just what
we ourselves, nourished on the Elizabethan tradition,
would naturally do. We should cut down the formal
speeches. We should not compel every speaker to
finish his verse. We should unhesitatingly drop the
god and the prologue and sometimes do without the
messenger. As for the Chorus, since we do not
know how to use it, we should cut it out altogether,
or, if that were impossible, cut it down to narrow
limits. We should work up the drama pure and
simple and forget the fixed lines of the ritual. We
should get rid of the monotonous shadow of death.
We should intermix tragedy and comedy. We should
aim at entertainment, at variety, not at worship.

There arose, after the fall of Tragedy, and of the
old unmixed Comedy, a form of drama which did all
these things. The New Comedy of Menander and
his predecessors introduced all the simplifications and
improvements which seem to a modern so obviously
desirable. It developed an easy colloquial language,
a flexible and unexacting metre. It left the Chorus

quite outside the play, a kind of *entr'acte*, not worth
writing down. It frankly abandoned religious ritual
and heroic saga. It drew its material from the adventures and emotions of contemporary middle-class life,
and boldly invented its own plots. And, as often
happens in matters of this sort, Fate was ironical.
Every single change seemed an obvious improvement
and the total result was an incomparable loss. It led
from the *Agamemnon* to the *Epitrepontes*.

When the end approached tragedy would make
no compromise. It turned its face deliberately back
towards its origin. Its last effort, the *Bacchae*, reads
almost like a defiance. It is a play drawn upon the
oldest and most rigid models; all about Dionysus,
all supernatural, all charged with ritual and mystery.
The speeches are long and formal, the scenes sharply
disconnected. The prologue, the god, the two
messengers are specially emphasized. Above all the
Chorus is the most dominant, the loveliest, the most
unearthly that had been seen on the Attic stage for
some two generations. The whole atmosphere of
the play is archaic; yet it was the last work of the
last master of Attic tragedy, and he was dead when
it was first acted. Its drama was not the drama
desired or understood by the younger generations,
yet when they looked at it they were fascinated. It
sprang at once into fame and held the stage continu-
ously to the end of antiquity, seeing other and easier
forms of drama rise and triumph and at last fall, a thing
never to be done again, scarcely to be understood,
recognized as the last witness to a beauty of which
the secret was lost and the ancient mould broken.

PLATONISM IN ENGLISH POETRY

By J. A. Stewart

WHEN I was honoured, at the end of last term, by being asked to lecture to you, this term, on 'Platonism in English Poetry', and agreed, perhaps too light-heartedly, to do so, I was aware that I was undertaking a difficult task; but, how difficult, I did not realize till it came to planning and writing; and now the upshot is that I am approaching you with the request that you will pardon me if, after some preliminary explanations which I shall make as brief as possible, I confine myself to a 'scanty plot of ground' within the wide area of our subject—to the poetry of Wordsworth, Coleridge, and Shelley.

It is a plot of ground, however, which, I would plead, has two great advantages to set off against its scantiness. First, it is a garden which we all already know and love; and our study of platonism within its enclosure will, at least, be sympathetic—a matter of the first importance where the understanding of an elusive spirit like that of platonism is concerned. Secondly, the platonism which our little garden offers to our study is, for the most part, what I would call 'personal platonism' only slightly affected by tradition; and it is personal platonism which, somehow or other, we must have learnt to appreciate, before we can hope to understand traditional platonism.

Let me begin the preliminary explanations, which I said would be as brief as possible, with what I am sure you wish me to begin with—with a statement of what platonism, as I understand it, is—and, more especially, of what it is as a spirit in poetry.

Platonism I would describe, in the most general terms, as the mood of one who has a curious eye for the endless variety of this visible and temporal world and a fine sense of its beauties, yet is haunted by the presence of an invisible and eternal world behind, or, when the mood is most pressing, within, the visible and temporal world, and sustaining both it and himself—a world not perceived as external to himself, but inwardly lived by him, as that with which, at moments of ecstasy, or even habitually, he is become one. This is how personal platonism, whether in a Plotinus or in a Wordsworth, may be described in outline—and it is in outline that such a mood is best described.

But traditional platonism enlarges, and adds detail to, the outline-description which is sufficient for personal platonism : and we are told that the man, who, in the temporal world, is haunted by the presence of the eternal world, is a Lover—that, from love of the visible and temporal, he is lifted up to love of the invisible and eternal world, of the existence of which his love is itself the sure evidence. Further, we are told that it is with its conjoined Ideas, or Powers, of Goodness, Truth, and Beauty, operating, for one end, through the agency of a hierarchy of dependent Ideas or Powers, that the world invisible and eternal—sometimes called World, sometimes God—sustains the world visible and temporal; sustains it, not once for all, but by continually creating it anew, always after its own likeness, but yet with endless variety, never the same. Further, we are told that the world so created is a living creature which has soul as well as body; and that it is through the intermediation of this created 'Soul of the World', or 'Plastic Spirit of Nature', that the operation of God, or of the eternal World of Ideas, actually reaches matter, and moulds it into the form of the world visible and temporal. Finally, we are told that the exaltation of love of the visible and temporal into that love which is evidence of the existence of the invisible and eternal world is inseparable from 'Recollection': the Lover had experience of the invisible and eternal world in a former life, and now in this life recollects it—sees it again, in flashes, through the darkness of the flesh.

This, in brief, is the teaching of traditional platonism.

With the psychology—as yet tentative—of the platonist mood, whether expressed in this teaching or otherwise, I will not trouble you. It is enough for us to know that the mood is a real experience. That it was an extraordinarily vivid experience in Plato himself is plain from the expression which he gives to it in the *Phaedrus*, *Symposium*, and *Timaeus* —an expression, indeed, so memorable that it arrested and held the attention of disciples almost to the exclusion of the Master's other teaching. Plato,

the great man of science, the mathematician, the
founder (along with Socrates) of logic and of moral
and political philosophy, was exploited and superseded by Aristotelians and Stoics, and soon ceased
to be an individual force even within his own
Academy. But Plato the prophet lived on in the
speculation of theologians, the inspiration of poets,
and the lives of religious men, Pagan, Jewish,
Christian, and Moslem, through the Alexandrine
period and the early centuries of our era, through
the dark ages so-called, through the two centuries
of the dawning renaissance, till in the latter half of
the fifteenth century, with the foundation of the
Platonic Academy at Florence, his personality became the object of a cult to which zeal for the new
learning, love of earthly beauty, and love of heavenly
beauty, all gave fervour. Plato's Dialogues, especially the *Phaedrus* and *Symposium*, as translated
and commented on by the chief devotee of this cult,
Marsilio Ficino, and the *Enneads* of Plotinus, as
translated by the same hand, now began to be
read in the West, and, while they influenced philosophy and theology chiefly, also influenced poetry
by adding volume and weight to a stream of
'Platonism' which could be traced back beyond
Dante, and, in the sonnets of Petrarch, more than
a century before the foundation of the Platonic
Academy, had already become a classic river which
was to flow on through Italian, French, and English
love-poetry—Spenser's, Sidney's, Shakespeare's, Jonson's, Drummond's, Donne's—till at last it was lost
in the confluence of other waters.

The platonism which lived throughout these eighteen or nineteen hundred years was, as I have said, not the doctrine of Plato the man of science, but the mood expressed in the *Phaedrus, Symposium,* and *Timaeus,* and that only—the mood of Plato the prophet, Plato's own expression of which, handed down by tradition, appealed to theologians and poets who already knew the mood as a personal experience of their own. Had there not been such personal experience to appeal to in an unbroken succession of men of genius, the platonic tradition could not have maintained itself even for the use of those who merely repeated its letter without understanding its spirit. In the main, throughout all these centuries, the platonism of the *Phaedrus, Symposium,* and *Timaeus* was a genuine faith—as in Philo the Jew, in Plotinus, in Erigena, in Dante, in Ficino himself, in Michael Angelo, in Spenser, in Cudworth, in Henry More. Only here and there, chiefly among sonneteers of the Petrarchan succession, did the platonism of these three Dialogues become a mannerism.

The platonism expressed in the *Phaedrus, Symposium,* and *Timaeus* is indeed a vital spirit not easily quenched. Its vitality seems to me to be bound up with what may be called its duality. It has two elements, logically distinguishable, which it holds in organic combination — love of the visible and temporal, and love of the invisible and eternal, the former love passing into the latter, not once for all, but, as it were, in a perennial stream. If love of the visible and temporal were ever to fail, love of the invisible and eternal would cease. It is only the born connoisseur of things seen and temporal who is likely to aspire to, and is able to attain to, and, without abating his love of things seen and temporal, is able to hold fast by that love, or faith, which is the certainty of things unseen and eternal.

I would ask you to note carefully this quality in platonism. Platonism is love of the unseen and eternal cherished by one who rejoices in the seen and temporal. This is the platonism of Plato himself, and, what concerns us especially now, it is the platonism which is vital in great poetry. But the history of platonism shows us how easily the continuity of the temporal with the eternal, of the visible with the invisible, may be broken, and two one-sided dead platonisms made out of the one living two-sided platonism. There were neoplatonic philosophers and theologians who preached only this: 'Shut your eyes to the visible that you may apprehend the invisible; flee from the flesh that you may find union with God'; and there were amorous sonneteers who were only platonists in manner, but, at heart, disciples of Ovid. After all, it is in the great poets, rather than in philosophers and theologians, that we find the balance of the platonist mood the more justly kept. The philosopher or theologian who is a platonist, unless he is endowed with great sensibility, is apt, as thinker, to treat Goodness, Truth, and Beauty, and the other Ideas dependent on them, as abstractions, for it is with abstractions that we think; whereas the great poet who is also a platonist is saved, by his poet's sensibility, from the extreme of asceticism, or abstraction, into which the theologian or philosopher is apt to fall. As poet, he is one who cannot take his eyes off the things of this visible world; and, as he looks intently at them, or vividly recalls them in solitary reflection, they charm him into dreaming them; he sees them with the eye, not of wayward fancy, but, since he is a born platonist, with the eye of steady imagination — sees them altered, on a sudden, into their own eternal meaning (I crave pardon for this hard saying)—sees them become vehicles of the unseen and eternal world which is substantially present in them behind the veil of their sensible attributes.

Now I have done with the preliminary explanations. You have, I trust, gathered from them, first, that it is to the great poets, rather than to philosophers and theologians (with some notable exceptions), that I would have you go for the finest expression of the platonist mood realized most adequately as a personal experience, and, secondly, that the study of this mood, as a personal experience expressed without the aid of traditional forms, ought to precede the study of it as expressed with the aid of them : for example (to take two platonist poets of the highest rank, Spenser and Wordsworth), we ought to study platonism in Wordsworth first, and then study it in Spenser.

I shall take Wordsworth and Coleridge closely together, in order to compare and contrast them as platonists.

In both the platonist mood is a personal experience little influenced by traditional platonic teaching, although, of course, that teaching was matter of knowledge to them. Both are aware of the real presence of the eternal in the temporal; the eternal for them is no abstraction apart, it is concretely present in the temporal: but Wordsworth is habitually aware of the real presence. Sometimes, indeed, it is ecstatically felt by him in 'gleams like the flashing of a shield',[1] but, for the most part, it is apprehended quietly in the actual scenes and occurrences, often quite ordinary scenes and occurrences, of external nature and of man's life directly observed, accurately remembered, and plainly described: whereas to Coleridge the presence of the eternal is only intermittently revealed. The cause of this difference is interesting, and helps us to understand the conditions under which the platonist mood is realized. As Wordsworth saw, Coleridge's was a mind 'debarred from nature's living images'[2] —debarred by 'its self-created sustenance', 'platonic forms', and 'words for things' (Wordsworth is speaking here of Coleridge at Cambridge)—'debarred from nature's living images' most of all, I would add, by an imagination, weird and romantic, and little moved by passion. 'Nature's living images,' actually existing, ordinary things, seen in mental pictures which fill us with wonder, although they are soberly, even austerely, drawn true to life— such is the world, seen and temporal, in which the mind of a Plato, or a Dante, or a Wordsworth is aware, and makes us aware, of the world unseen and

---

[1] *Prelude*, i.   [2] *Prelude*, vi.

eternal. Debarred from this world of living images
by his weird and romantic imagination, Coleridge
produced, in the *Ancient Mariner* and *Christabel,*
what is, doubtless, great poetry—great, because it
translates us, with amazement, from this earth ; but
not the very greatest poetry, because it is not to
the Platonic Plain of Truth, not to the unmoved
Empyrean Heaven that it translates us, only to the
space, midway between the Earth and the Moon,
where the demon-heroes and the fairies are. And
Coleridge was a great poet only in his youth—only
so long as the pageant of weird images still kept
passing before him. The time came to him pre-
maturely when the ' self-created sustenance' of his
mind failed, and he could say :

> Afflictions bow me down to earth :
> Nor care I that they rob me of my mirth,
> But oh ! each visitation
> Suspends what nature gave me at my birth,
> My shaping spirit of Imagination.

While Imagination remained he was content with
fairyland, and heeded not the world unseen and
eternal : but when Imagination failed, then he longed
for the world unseen and eternal, and sought it where
his memory of rare ecstatic moments told him it is
to be found, in ' nature's living images '—in the world
seen and temporal pictured, as it is, for our wonder :
but he sought in vain, for the Dejection which sus-
pended his shaping spirit of Imagination also killed
the inward joy out of which, in the past, these ecstatic
moments had flashed :

All this long eve, so balmy and serene,
Have I been gazing on the western sky,
And its peculiar tint of yellow green :
And still I gaze—and with how blank an eye!
And those thin clouds above, in flakes and bars,
That give away their motion to the stars ;
Those stars, that glide behind them or between,
Now sparkling, now bedimmed, but always seen ;
Yon crescent moon as fixed as if it grew
In its own cloudless, starless, lake of blue ;
I see them all so excellently fair,
I see, not feel, how beautiful they are !

To see, and while one sees, to feel Beauty—this is
the platonist mood. That the mood which Coleridge
here—in *Dejection : an Ode*—so pathetically mourns
as gone from him, was his at times, and was experienced in the contemplation of 'nature's living
images', let the two following passages testify :
This (addressed to Charles Lamb, in *This lime-tree
bower my prison*) :

                    Ah ! slowly sink
Behind the western ridge, thou glorious sun !
Shine in the slant beams of the sinking orb,
Ye purple heath-flowers ! richlier burn, ye clouds !
Live in the yellow light, ye distant groves !
And kindle, thou blue ocean ! So my Friend
Struck with deep joy may stand, as I have stood,
Silent with swimming sense ; yea, gazing round
On the wide landscape, gaze till all doth seem
Less gross than bodily ; and of such hues
As veil the Almighty Spirit, when yet he makes
Spirits perceive his presence—

and this (in the *Eolian Harp*) :

O the one life within us and abroad,
Which meets all motion and becomes its soul,

A light in sound, a sound-like power in light,
Rhythm in all thought, and joyance everywhere—
Methinks it should have been impossible
Not to love all things in a world so filled ;
Where the breeze warbles, and the mute still air
Is music slumbering on her instrument.

. . . .

And what if all of animated nature
Be but organic harps diversely framed,
That tremble into thought, as o'er them sweeps
Plastic and vast, one intellectual breeze,
At once the soul of each, and God of all.

In *The Prelude, or Growth of a Poet's Mind, an
Autobiographical Poem,* Wordsworth produced a work
which must be regarded as the classic authority on
Platonism in Poetry. The essential nature and the
necessary conditions of the platonist mood, as
experienced by one who is a poet, are set forth by
Wordsworth, in the *Prelude*, with so much first-hand
knowledge, and with such subtlety of analysis and
completeness of circumstance, that, if I might venture
to offer advice, I would say that the study of this poem
ought to precede the study of platonism in other
English poets—especially where the platonism is much
influenced by tradition, as it is in Spenser, and his
successors, whether leaning to the Ovidian or to the
'metaphysical' side in style. I would have you
make the platonist mood revealed as a personal
experience in the *Prelude* the touchstone of the
genuineness of the platonism ostensibly present in
the writings of any one of this line of poets.

Let me, then, put down some of the marks of the

platonist mood as Wordsworth helps us in the *Prelude* to surmise its nature.

It is an 'amplitude of mind'—to use an expression which occurs in *Prelude* xiv—which may be called indifferently Love, Imagination, Reason—an amplitude of mind which the eternal world, present within the temporal world, fills with its influence. In the first place, figured as *Love* the mood is an experience in which a Beauty not of this world suddenly flashes through the transparency of some scene or event of this world, and entering into the poet's heart and cherished there, becomes a habit which disposes him ever after to recall the scene or event, and other scenes and events like it, and see them illumined with 'glory not their own'. But, secondly, thus habitually to recall and see is *Imagination*, which does not change the scene or event, as Fancy does, into something else, but sees it steadily as it is, only illumined: so that, while remaining the same scene or event for description, it is become, for imagination, the symbol of some Power or Virtue, or, as Plato would say, Idea, in which the diffused Beauty of the eternal world takes specific form. And, thirdly, the platonist mood, being Love and Imagination, is also *Reason*—the intuitive apprehension of the one spiritual system of the universe, which Love seeks after as Heavenly Beauty sojourning on earth, and Imagination sees variously figured in scenes and events of this temporal world become symbols:

> I held unconscious intercourse with beauty
> Old as creation.

        All that I beheld
Was dear, and hence to finer influxes
The mind lay open, to a more exact
And close communion.

          I would walk alone,
Under the quiet stars, and at that time
Have felt whate'er there is of power in sound
To breathe an elevated mood, by form
Or image unprofaned ; and I would stand,
If the night blackened with a coming storm,
Beneath some rock, listening to notes that are
The ghostly language of the ancient earth,
Or make their dim abode in distant winds.
Thence did I drink the visionary power ;
And deem not profitless those fleeting moods
Of shadowy exultation : not for this,
That they are kindred to our purer mind
And intellectual life ; but that the soul
Remembering how she felt, but what she felt
Remembering not, retains an obscure sense
Of possible sublimity, whereto
With growing faculties she doth aspire,
With faculties still growing, feeling still
That whatsoever point they gain, they yet
Have something to pursue.
             And not alone,
'Mid gloom and tumult, but no less 'mid fair
And tranquil scenes, that universal power
And fitness in the latent qualities
And essences of things, by which the mind
Is moved with feelings of delight, to me
Came strengthened with a superadded soul,
A virtue not its own.

   .   .   .   .

How shall I seek the origin ? where find
Faith in the marvellous things which then I felt ?

Oft in these moments such a holy calm
Would overspread my soul, that bodily eyes
Were utterly forgotten, and what I saw
Appeared like something in myself, a dream,
A prospect in the mind.

This from the *Prelude*; the following from *The
Wye above Tintern*.

I have felt
A presence that disturbs me with the joy
Of elevated thoughts; a sense sublime
Of something far more deeply interfused,
Whose dwelling is the light of setting suns,
And the round ocean and the living air,
And the blue sky, and in the mind of man :
A motion and a spirit, that impels
All thinking things, all objects of all thought,
And rolls through all things. Therefore am I still
A lover of the meadows and the woods,
And mountains; and of all that we behold
From this green earth.

From these passages (and there are many like
them in the *Excursion*, in the *Intimations of Immortality*, and throughout the whole poetry of Wordsworth) we can surmise what the personal platonism
of a great poet necessarily is. First, for him the
eternal is immanent in the temporal, not transcendent
as it may be for the philosopher and theologian, if
they lack a poet's sensibility. Secondly, the immanence is at first revealed in flashes to the poet—
and here a poet may stop, and yet be a great poet.
But, thirdly, the greatest poets are those to whom, as
to Wordsworth, the immanence, at first revealed in
flashes, becomes, in course of time, the object of an

habitual faith, as we may call it, which dominates their lives, so that in the end they see all things, great and small, *sub specie aeternitatis,* as symbols. For them the temporal world is become altogether a scheme of symbols :

Alles Vergängliche ist nur ein Gleichniss.

Here let me say something about symbolism, for I think that, by doing so, I may make clearer to you what I understand by the personal platonism of a great poet.

Symbols are of two kinds : first, those invented and made by the poet himself or his predecessors ; and, secondly, those which are not invented and made at all, but come of themselves to the individual poet —spontaneous symbols, we may call them.

The study of invented symbols belongs mainly to the domain of literary history. The main task of the student is to explain the structure of certain similes and personifications, and to interpret certain allegories, as they occur; and this he does by reading the intended ' meaning ' of each in the light of its literary history.

As for spontaneous symbols, the symbols which are not invented at all, but come of themselves, the first and last thing to be said about them is that they have no literary history and do not admit of interpretation. They spring, without the poet's conscious aid, out of his emotion. They are of two sorts, according as their form is supplied mainly by external nature, or is mainly the product of the poet's entranced brain : that is, spontaneous symbols—symbols which are not invented, but come—are to be distinguished as nature's symbols, and trance-symbols. Nature's symbols are what Wordsworth calls ' nature's living images'—actual scenes, or events, or persons, accurately pictured by the poet in tranquillity, with the after-light upon them of a vivid emotion which his first seeing or picturing of them kindled in him : it is this after-light which transforms them from mere memory-images into symbols. Such symbols do not admit of being 'interpreted'. What 'interpretation' is possible or needed of the scene which Wordsworth saw with the eye of Love, or of Imagination, or of 'the more-than-reasoning mind ',[1] when he wrote

> Flow on for ever, Yarrow stream !
> Fulfil thy pensive duty,
> Well pleased that future bards should chaunt
> For simple hearts thy beauty :
> To dream-light dear while yet unseen,
> Dear to the common sunshine,
> And dearer still, as now I feel,
> To memory's shadowy moonshine !

This dear image is a symbol which is itself its own meaning, and needs no further interpretation.

And so too it is with the other sort of spontaneous symbols, with trance-symbols, images, like Ezekiel's, or Dante's, or Vaughan's—'I saw Eternity the other night'—images with no definite external originals, which flash spontaneously out of some tense emotional state of the poet, especially when ordinary outlets are closed, and, relieving for a moment—just as an involuntary cry or gesture may relieve—the tension of the emotion, are accepted straightway as

---

[1] *Misc. Sonnets*, Part I, Son. xxxv.

'interpreting' the mystery with which the emotion
is charged—how, words cannot tell : for the trance-
image, thus become a symbol, is, like nature's symbol,
itself the 'interpretation' longed for, and admits of no
further interpretation ; the mere seeing it with the
mind's eye, or hearing it with the mind's ear, is the
'interpretation' eagerly expected. The emotional
tension is a sort of ineffable question, and here is
the answer to it!—this loud shout of praise heard afar,
articulating itself, as Dante listens, into melody and
words (*Par.* xiv, xxiv) ; this sudden illumination in
which the bright forms shape themselves before his
eyes when he first has sight of the Celestial Rose
(*Par.* xxx–xxxiii). These are the modes, well known
to the psychologist, in which tense religious, or other,
feeling expresses itself ; and it is in connexion with
these experiences that the need of symbolic expression, and its primary satisfaction by means of the
spontaneous symbol, must be accounted for. The
need of symbolic expression, first naturally satisfied
by the spontaneous symbol, and then artificially by the
invented symbol embroidered, if it is to have any poetic
value, on the web of the spontaneous symbol—this
need of symbolic expression is involved in the very
nature of emotion, which is a state of tension always
seeking relief in cries, in gestures, or (and it is this
that concerns us here) in images, either nature's
living images—natural objects seen pictured with the
after-light upon them—or trance-images.

You see already, I trust, why I have dwelt on the
spontaneous symbols—the symbols which are not invented by the poet, but come to him of themselves.

I have done so, because, when such symbols appear in the Wordsworthian form of 'nature's living images', they are just what the platonist mood is aware of as objects of sense informed with the *parusia*, the real presence, of the Beauty, in its various specific forms, of the eternal world. The sole meaning of one of 'nature's living images'—Yarrow unvisited, Yarrow visited, Yarrow revisited—is simply itself, as the poet sees it, with 'the hope divine of pure imagination'[1] quickened by it in his heart. Here 'resemblance' between symbol and thing symbolized is not to be thought of, for each belongs to a different world. The symbol is the image of an object of sense in the temporal world, the thing symbolized is in the eternal world, beyond sense, beyond understanding; not seen, not known, but felt: the poet's sole guarantee of its reality is 'the hope divine of pure imagination', felt while he pictures Yarrow, or Wye, The Highland Girl, or Michael building the sheep-fold on the foundation sacramentally laid by his son.

Wordsworth's poetry, then, being impassioned contemplation of 'nature's living images', takes rank as a typical product of the platonist mood. For this mood, Beauty, Truth, and Goodness, and the other Powers or Ideas of the eternal world, are always substantially present in objects of sense, never exist apart as abstractions waiting, like all abstractions, to be personified and to have their parts assigned to them, as persons or puppets, in some elaborated allegory. It is a mistake to suppose, as some have done, that deliberate personification and

[1] *Excursion*, v.

allegory are of the essence of platonism. They were, indeed, introduced into platonism at an early time—against the precept of Plato himself, and, since his myths are not allegories, against his example too—and became traditional, as exegetical methods in theology, and embellishments in poetry; but they are really, in so far as they are deliberately invented, foreign to its nature. As soon as Goodness, Truth, Beauty, and the other Ideas of the eternal world are deliberately personified, and have parts carefully assigned to them in allegory, they are become mere items in a pageant of the temporal world—objects which Fancy plays with. But for a poet like Wordsworth there is nothing to personify and play with : ' nature's living images ', informed with the presence of the eternal world, are already there, and are, themselves, sufficient. The more pressing the platonist mood is in such a poet, the more directly and simply, eschewing simile, personification, and allegory, will he describe the objects and events of the world of external nature and of man's life which constitute the matter of his poem. He will describe these objects and events directly and simply, because they themselves were just what he had before him in sense or memory, when, on a sudden, he felt ' the hope divine of pure imagination ' in his heart, and the presence of the eternal world encompassed him. To alter these objects or events by personification, or allegory, or simile, would be to trifle with the august experience which came to him while he regarded them.

Now we come to personal platonism in Shelley;

and what I have just said about the incompatibility
of allegory and personification with the genuine
platonist mood may make you think that I ought
to say that there is no personal platonism in Shelley.
But I am not going to say that :

> That garden sweet, that lady fair,
> And all sweet shapes and odours there
> In truth have never passed away :
> 'Tis we, 'tis our's, are changed ! not they.

> For love, and beauty, and delight,
> There is no death, nor change; their might
> Exceeds our organs, which endure
> No light, being themselves obscure.

These concluding lines of *The Sensitive Plant*
breathe the genuine spirit of personal platonism,
but such lines are comparatively rare in Shelley ; and
his poetry, as a whole, with its abounding personification of the modes of human thought, feeling, and
action, and of the phenomena of external nature,
gives little evidence of the influence of the platonist
mood likely, at first sight, to be satisfactory to any
one who takes Wordsworth as the Platonist Poet
par excellence. It is in these modes and phenomena
themselves, as they are, not as changed by personification into what they are not, that the platonist mood,
as exhibited by Wordsworth finds what it seeks.

But we must not judge Shelley's platonism by
the standard of Wordsworth's. There is all the difference in the world between deliberate personification, which is, indeed, foreign to the genius of
platonism, as debarring us from nature's living
images, and spontaneous personification. Sponta-

neous personification is simply Shelley's way of
seeing nature's living images. Sometimes his
visionary personages are tender dream-shapes,
dryads and naiads, who for him, as for the old
Greek countrymen, at once are, and are not, the
very oak-trees and fountains; more often his personification is, like Blake's, of elemental powers, the
might of which passes in passion through his sympathetic soul, and embodies itself in Titanic forms.
How different is such personification from that
which, in the professedly platonist poetry of the
Petrarchan tradition, so often but ill conceals the
entire absence of personal platonism! Shelley's
skilful and learned Fancy, indeed, clothes his visionary personages with newly invented or traditional
attributes: but behind the added attributes, the
visionary personages themselves are always there,
not invented, but come of themselves out of the
poet's day-dream or passion; and they are, for him,
what images of actual scenes and events and persons
are for Wordsworth, visible and temporal vehicles of
the invisible and eternal. Read Wordsworth's sonnet
beginning, 'Even so for me a vision sanctified,' and
Shelley's *Adonaïs* together, and you will feel assured
that this is so: the eternal world which Love discerns
present in this world is not less manifest to Shelley
in the visionary personages who throng the Roman
chamber where Keats lies dead, than it is to Wordsworth in the face which he describes so simply:

When thou, dear Sister! wert become Death's Bride,
No trace of pain or languor could abide

That change:—age on thy brow was smoothed—thy
    cold
Wan cheek at once was privileged to unfold
A loveliness to living youth denied.
Oh! if within me hope should e'er decline,
The lamp of faith, lost Friend! too faintly burn ;
Then may that heaven-revealing smile of thine,
The bright assurance, visibly return :
And let my spirit in that power divine
Rejoice, as, through that power, it ceased to mourn.

We may say, then, that personification, which is
certainly not essential to platonism, and is a weakness
in the majority of platonist poets, is the strength
of Shelley's platonism : these visionary personages
spring spontaneously out of his ecstatic passion, out
of his longing to be made one with the Spirit of
Nature, which is the Spirit of Beauty. It is in a
fairy chariot, moving in a pageant of such visionary
personages, that the ascension is made, in *Queen
Mab*, to the Temple of this Spirit, just as the
ascension to the Plain of Truth is made by winged
chariots in the *Phaedrus* :

> Spirit of Nature! here!
> In this interminable wilderness
>   Of worlds, at whose immensity
>   Even soaring fancy staggers,
>   Here is thy fitting temple.
>   Yet not the lightest leaf
> That quivers to the passing breeze
>   Is less instinct with thee :
>   Yet not the meanest worm
> That lurks in graves and fattens on the dead
> Less shares thy eternal breath.
> Spirit of Nature! thou!

> Imperishable as this scene,
> Here is thy fitting temple!

And in the *Hymn to Intellectual Beauty*, he tells us that his life was early dedicated to the service of this Spirit, which

> —visits with inconstant glance
> Each human heart and countenance;
> Like hues and harmonies of evening,
> Like clouds in starlight widely spread,
> Like memory of music fled,
> Like aught that for its grace may be
> Dear, and yet dearer for its mystery.
>
> Spirit of BEAUTY! . . . .
> .   .   .   .
> I vowed that I would dedicate my powers
> To thee and thine: have I not kept the vow?

I must now end, as I began, with apology. I have left alone, not only English poetry before Spenser which was influenced by platonism, but the line, after him, of English poets distinctively called platonist, in whose poetry, whether amorous or religious, the whole apparatus of traditional platonism is displayed —Intelligible world, Eternal Ideas recollected in this life from the experience of a former life, Eternal Beauty, chief among these Ideas, discerned by Intellectual Love, the so-called 'Platonic Love', which is the perfection of the love engendered in the eye of sense by gazing on earthly beauty. All these poets, with this apparatus, I have left alone, that I might persuade you also to leave them alone until you have found the touchstone which shall test the quality of their platonism—until you have learnt from Wordsworth, and Coleridge, and Shelley, especially from Wordsworth, what personal as distinguished from traditional platonism is—learnt this from Wordsworth, and in learning it from him, have found out, perhaps, that you yourselves have been platonists all your lives, without knowing it.

And just another word more before I end. You understand, I am sure, that the distinction which I have so continually spoken of, using Platonic language, between World invisible and eternal and World visible and temporal, is a distinction with which scientific thought has no concern : it is a distinction which is valid only within the region where Poetry reigns : but it is not therefore of less moment to us in the conduct of our lives.

THEOPHRASTUS AND HIS IMITATORS

By G. S. Gordon

Theophrastus, I may say at once, was the founder of the science of Botany. This is his greatest title to fame, and for one man it might seem to be enough. Yet I venture to think that you would be surprised if this should prove to be a lecture on his fifteen surviving books on the Natural History and Physiology of Plants, and if, when I spoke of his imitators, I spoke of Linnaeus and the Darwins. Theophrastus has had the fate of many great men and great workers, to be best remembered by the slightest of his performances. His little series of Character-sketches was the leisure amusement of perhaps the hardest-working and most voluminous philosopher of the ancient world ; it is, however, precisely that part of him which the world still wishes, and has always wished, to read. I hope that, while we remark this incongruity, we are none of us surprised at it ; to be surprised at such things is to have read the history of literature in vain. The quarrel between labour and love is the oldest quarrel in the world, and the first cause of that gallant uncertainty and gamble of the arts which no artist, even while he curses it, would wish away. Look where you will among the nations of authors, how frequent it is : Boethius, the indefatigable commentator, remem-

bered only by a prison tract; John Selden, profound-
est of scholars and wits, living only in his table-talk;
Thomas Gray, the filler of note-books and very
leach of learning of his age, known to the general
world as the author of an elegy of some hundred
lines. Charles Lamb, who felt most things, felt this
also, looking with those humorous eyes of his at the
massive ledgers, *his* ledgers, in the India House,
'more MSS. in folio than ever Aquinas left'—my
'works!', he calls them: his essays were only play.
In this secular triumph of spirit over matter the
world is as heartless and as healthy as a child.
Time and trouble and all the rest of the author's
ritual, it cares nothing for them; to hit it between
wind and water the projectile must be volatile, it
must fly. The moral of Theophrastus's fate would
seem to be this, that professors are admired in their
own day for their learning, but at the last for their
jeux d'esprit.

I said professors, because Theophrastus was a
professor. He was the head of the Aristotelian
College in Athens. He succeeded Aristotle in the
school of philosophy which Aristotle had founded,
and carried on the work for nearly forty years, dying
at a legendary age about 284 B. C. It was a pleasant
life for a scholar. The School of the Peripatetics
was much like an Oxford college. It had its chapel,
its cloisters, its hall, its garden, its library, its walks,
and its president's lodgings; the students lived
close by, and held gaudies from time to time, according to rules (ξυμποτικοὶ νόμοι) laid down by Aristotle,
the first head, as Ben Jonson laid down the rules at

the Mermaid. In this society Theophrastus worked incessantly, lecturing, discussing, writing; students came in crowds; he carried on without servility the whole tradition of Aristotle, and was notable in every department of philosophy. The man himself seems to have been of a generous and vivacious nature, passing into urbanity with age. Every morning, says Hermippus, 'bright and early, Theophrastus would appear at the place of lecture, finely groomed and apparelled, and taking his seat, proceed to discourse with such perfect abandon of movement and gesture that on one occasion, to illustrate a description he was giving of the Gourmand, he put out his tongue and licked his lips before the whole assembly' (Athen. I. 21 a). His greatest enemy was time. He died wishing for more, and grudged, says Cicero, the dispensation of nature which had given deer and crows so many years of life of which they could make no use, and so few to man, who, were his life but longer, might hope to reach at last the universal science.

His *Characters* are a work of his later years. They were written in the last quarter of the fourth century before Christ; one or two can be dated exactly to the year 319. It was not a year in which Athenians could be very proud of themselves, with a Macedonian garrison in the Peiraeus, and more than half of their 21,000 citizens transported out of Attica. This Athens of Theophrastus was no longer the seat of an empire; it was soon to be little more than a municipality with a past, famous for its buildings, its statues, its Greek, and its schools. Its citizens—such citizens are were left—took to minding their private concerns and considering the vanity of human wishes. Denied the exhilarating study of national questions, they fell back on the narrower study of their neighbours. Denied the macrocosm, they turned instead to the microcosm of municipal man. To instruct and amuse this municipal society Theophrastus invented the Character, and Menander, his pupil in philosophy, perfected the Comedy of Manners. It is a significant conjunction, not peculiar to Athens. You will find that whenever Characters are written there is this same conjunction, of Character-writing and Comedy: to every Theophrastus his Menander. To Hall, Overbury, and Earle, the accepted imitators of Theophrastus in England, corresponds Ben Jonson with his Comedy of Humours, an earlier, harsher, and profounder version of the later Comedy of Manners. To La Bruyère, his professed disciple in France, corresponds the comedy of Molière, the French Menander. To the *Tatler* and *Spectator*, the New Testament, as I may call them, of Character-writing in England, corresponds the comedy of Congreve, our English Molière. They go together, you observe, naturally, like members of one family, and we are tempted to ask which is the elder and points the way. It is a question not often asked. For the moment let us rest in the certainty that they are contemporaries and express the same instinct. They are both the voice of a society to which nothing is so interesting as the spectacle of itself.

There is another conjunction to be noted. The

representation of manners always supposes some
philosophy of conduct, some standard by which we
judge, and some method of discovering it. In such a
society as I have indicated the method will generally
be the same; Aristotle had only put it into form
when he laid down his doctrine of the Mean. This
doctrine is at the root of Theophrastus's *Characters*,
and is everywhere implied by such comedies as
Menander's. The *Characters* of Theophrastus are,
indeed, an artistic by-product of a long pre-occupation
with the terms of conduct. From the start the most
popular task of the Aristotelian ethics was to define
these terms. Virtue once admitted to be the mean,
it became necessary to define all the extremes, the
too little and too much of the social appearances of
man. Aristotle had exhibited the method in his
Ethics, and handed over the results to the rhetoricians
in his *Rhetoric*; it was the part of his successors
to keep the application up to date, since social
terms are always changing their meaning. Αὐθάδεια,
which Aeschylus thought adequate to the Prome-
thean self-will, has sunk in Theophrastus to a
commonplace surliness, a transition hardly greater
than we ourselves have witnessed from the social
language of the eighteenth century, when a soul and
a tea-party might equally be 'elegant', and husbands
mourned the loss of 'valuable' wives. So the game
of distinguishing went steadily, I will not say merrily
on. Eudemus and Theophrastus are busy at it in
the age of Alexander, and all the imitators of
Theophrastus up to Philodemus of Gadara, in the
age of Cicero and Caesar.

This conjunction of Character-writing and philosophy, like that other conjunction of which I spoke, is not peculiar to the ancients. The Characters of Hall and Earle, like the comedies of Ben Jonson, are founded on a theory of human nature which had at any rate the authority of the physicians, a theory as old as Galen, the theory of Humours. On this theory the Hamlets are judged by the Horatios, and found wanting. In France, in the age of La Bruyère, Horatio is Horace, *l'honnête homme*; he sums up the ethics of the age and is equally at the root of La Bruyère's Characters and Molière's comedies. Put 'man of sense' for *l'honnête homme*, and what better basis will you find for the social portraiture of Addison and Congreve? On the order and more intimate relation of these several expressions of the social spirit, I shall have something to say later. There is no doubt that they feed on one another, and that in the adjustment of the banquet Comedy has generally given more than she has received. In the meantime I am content to enforce these two conjunctions, to be found in each appearance of the Theophrastian spirit, of Character-writing with a Comedy of Manners, and of a Moral Philosophy with both. If you consider them, it will appear very natural that Theophrastus and Menander should have been contemporaries, and that the first examples of what we call Characters should have been written by the representative of the Aristotelian ethics of the Mean.

They were written, I imagine, as much for amusement as for profit, to enliven the classroom, and were handed about in copies, like Overbury's and

Earle's. It is this that makes them new. To describe social types as illustrations of the doctrine of the Mean was a stock exercise of the Aristotelian school of which its founder had bequeathed some memorable examples ; it was left for Theophrastus to cut the doctrine and give the picture for itself. This is his achievement, and this, I need not remind you, is art. In this passage from doctrine to art Theophrastus was assisted by the needs of the schools. The business of the Character was not wholly ethical ; in recalling its ethical origin we must not forget its rhetorical end. The classroom for which Theophrastus wrote I take to have been the classroom of rhetoric, in which the student, throwing off the moralist, emerged as the persuader of men, and passed from the defining of types to the description of them. This description of types must always have held an honourable place in the art of Rhetoric, an art which depends so much more than most arts on the lively depicting and discrimination of character. When we have compared, therefore, the *Characters* of Theophrastus with the analyses of character in Aristotle's *Ethics*, and remarked the absence of that application of the Mean by which Aristotle interrupts his sketches, we have done something interesting and necessary, but we have missed the ford. To make the passage from the *Ethics* to the *Characters* we must go by way of the *Rhetoric*,[1] in which the place of pure ἤθη or Character-

---

[1] Cp. espec. III. 16. 9, where a telegraphic example is given of the kind of thing wanted : οἷον ὅτι ἅμα λέγων ἐβάδιζεν κτλ., ' As if you said, " And as he walked he threw the words over his shoulder,"—a sure mark of the Swaggerer or the Boor.'

drawing in the equipment of the orator is illustrated and defined. Such as these ἤθη were intended to be, such are the Characters of Theophrastus. Saturated as they are with the Aristotelian ethics, their immediate motive, like most of their subsequent history, is rhetorical; and this explains, among other things, how easily Theophrastus came to invent them.

There are thirty of these Characters left, and they have a common method. They start with a definition of some term of social blame—Fussiness, Boorishness, Meanness, Tactlessness, and the like—and proceed to a catalogue of the sort of thing the corresponding person will do or say. The formula never varies: τοιοῦτός τις οἷος, 'the sort of person who'; and then a string of infinitives describing actions. Thus:

The Boor

Boorishness should seem to be a clownish ignorance of propriety. The Boor is one who will take a drench and then go into the Ecclesia. He vows that garlic smells sweeter than any perfume ; he wears shoes too large for his feet; he talks in a loud voice. He distrusts his friends and relatives, but talks confidentially to his own servants on the most important matters ; and recounts all the news from the Ecclesia to the hired men working on his land. Wearing a cloak which does not reach to the knee, he will sit down. . . . He shows surprise and wonder at nothing else, but will stand still and gaze when he sees an ox or an ass or a goat in the streets. He has a way of taking things out of the store-room and eating them, and drinking his wine rather strong. He will help the bakery-wench to grind the corn for the use of the household and himself, after trying to put his arms round her.[1]   He will eat his breakfast while he shakes down hay for his beasts; he will answer the door himself, and call the dog to him, and take him by the nose, saying, 'This fellow looks after the place and the house.'   When he is given a piece of money, he will reject it because it is 'too worn', and take another instead; and if he has lent his plough, or a basket or sickle or bag, and remembers it as he lies awake, he will ask it back in the middle of the night.   On his way down to Athens he will ask the first man he meets how hides and salt fish were selling, and whether the magistrate celebrates the New Moon to-day, adding immediately that he means to have his hair cut when he gets to town, and at the same visit to fetch some salt fish from Archias as he goes by. He will also sing at the bath; and will drive nails into his shoes.[2]

It is a simple method; plain black and white. The author is out of it.   There are no colours and no explanations.   The language is the simplest possible, neither bookish nor doctrinal nor contro-versial.   The gloomy desire to show reading, which devoured our men of the seventeenth century, *l'envie de faire des sentences* which devoured the French, is wholly absent from his pages.   He relies for his effect on the simplicity of truth.   Every folly is reduced to its simplest terms and put before you without, as it were, a word said.   When you laugh, it is at humour in its last element of simple incongruity. There is the Unpleasant Man ($\dot{a}\eta\delta\eta\varsigma$), who 'remarks in an encouraging tone over the wine that the amuse-

---

[1] Adopting Diels's attractive conjecture, $\pi\epsilon\rho\iota\lambda\alpha\beta\epsilon\hat{\iota}\nu$.
[2] Ἀγροικίας δ'.   The translations are based on Jebb's.

ment of the company has been provided for'; the
Fussy Well-meaning Man (περίεργος), who says to the
bystanders when he is about to take an oath, 'This
is by no means the first oath I have taken'; the
Shameless Man (ἀναίσχυντος), who, when he goes
marketing, reminds the butcher of any little services
he may have done him; the Loquacious Man (λάλος),
who says, 'How much one gets from a little talk, to
be sure!' and whose children say to him, at bedtime,
'Papa, chatter to us, that we may fall asleep'; the
Late-learner (ὀψιμαθής), poor toiler after Music and
Gymnastic, who 'has a way of wriggling like
a wrestler when he is at the bath, in order that he
may appear educated, and, when women are near,
falls to practising steps to his own warble'. There
is also the man who replies, when some one brings
him the good news 'A son is born to you'—'If you
add that I have lost half my property you will be
speaking the truth.' This man, I need hardly say,
is the Grumbler (μεμψίμοιρος).

This reliance on truth is combined with a very
keen and unobtrusive art. The transitions of the
Garrulous Man, the devices of the Coward, the inconsequences of the Stupid Man, who, if he be asked
'How many corpses do you suppose have been
carried out at the Sacred Gate?' will say 'I only
wish that you or I had as many'—the author seems
to have nothing to do with them. The transitions,
the devices, the inconsequences are all in nature.
Such a method refuses wit. Theophrastus is witty
on his own account only once or twice, and then by
a word. The Late-learner has matches at archery

and javelin-throwing with his children's attendant, and exhorts him to learn from *him*—'as if', says Theophrastus, 'the other knew nothing about it *either.*' The Unseasonable Man (ἄκαιρος) is the sort of person who, 'when he takes it into his head to dance, will catch hold of another person *who is not yet drunk.*' I confess that every time I look at the shameless unchristened wit of our Overburys, Clevelands, and Butlers, I have a greater admiration for the artistic economy of Theophrastus. For whatever else we may be, however stormy, magnificent, and profound, we are poor economists in art. Theophrastus looks like a primitive beside the flaming oils of most of the English writers, but he has everything he wants. His effects are less ambitious, but they are certain, and good for every age.

Theophrastus had two great advantages over the Englishmen. He had, in the first place, a perfectly defined method and a perfectly defined set of terms. The training in the Aristotelian trios, mean and two extremes, makes his line sure. He will give you three parallel characters and keep them parallel, without a single intersection. The Penurious, the Mean, and the Avaricious Man—many of the things they do are and must be the same; all that the author allows himself is to say what they do; yet the same actions seem to carry a different meaning in each. What any one else would have done by explanation he does by mere subtlety of order and juxtaposition. When the Penurious Man collects the scraps, we feel that it is only economy pushed too far; when the Mean Man does it, we feel that he is shabby because he must know that he can afford to give something away ; when the Avaricious Man does it, we feel that it is the act of a maniac to whom nothing is sacred. Every action is shaded by another action, just before it or behind. The man might walk straight on to the stage, or into a novel, because he takes only his habitual actions with him. You could say that of few of the English Characters. Strip them of what is not their own—their author's wit—and there is really very little left to do anything. They have literally hardly a leg to stand on.

The other advantage which Theophrastus enjoyed was the combination of a very civilized with a very simple society : a community of the most active social sense, with its ideals in the past and its thoughts in the present, wholly occupied with the question how to live comfortably, conformably, and if possible elegantly. Nothing could be more parochial than the life which Theophrastus describes. Athens was very severe about deportment. 'Nicobulus', said Demosthenes, 'is an unpopular man ; he walks fast, talks loud, and carries a walking-stick.' The length of one's cloak, the length of one's hair, were watched with equal strictness. The Oligarchic Man, the member of the Upper Ten, was careful to have his hair just the right length : μέσην κουρὰν κεκαρμένος, the middle length : the Mean, in fact, even here. Petty Ambition is blamed for having his hair cut too often, as Philosophers for keeping it too long ; for keeping his teeth white, as the Disgusting Man for keeping them black ; for using unguent, when ordinary people used plain olive oil. There were all sorts of things that a family keeping its head up must not do. To answer the hall door yourself was one of them: you must never do that; and on the whole it was not the thing to do your own marketing. There were all sorts of petty rivalries, too, in the seats you took at the theatre, and the scale of your household. When you had sacrificed an ox, it was not unnatural to nail up a piece of the skin by the entrance of your house to let people know that you *had* sacrificed an ox. Mixed with the rivalry of household with household, there is a strange community in their lives. They are always borrowing things from next door: a little barley, or a lamp-wick, or some salt. And a strange publicity too. It is noted against the Arrogant Man (ὑπερήφανος) that he refuses to see visitors when he is anointing himself, or sitting at table, or having his bath. Consider, if this be Arrogance, how far we have travelled from Humility! It is to be observed, also, that they are as exact as the Scotch about funerals, and that nearly everybody sends his cloak to the fuller's to be cleaned.

In this society there is much easy family life. The children come in quite often. It is a mark of the Toady (κόλαξ) that he buys apples and pears to give to them in front of their father, and of the Man who Tries to Please Everybody (ἄρεσκος) that he will ask his host to send for them at dinner, and declare when they come in that they are as like their father as figs, and draw them to him and kiss them, playing with some of them and saying over the nursery refrain of 'Wineskin', 'Hatchet', and permitting others to go to sleep upon him, to his agony (ἅμα θλιβόμενος). This air of nature in the amusements of the children did not extend, alas, to the amusements of their elders. You were expected to sing and make verses after dinner, or, if you would not sing, at least to recite. It is remarked of the young blood in the *Clouds* of Aristophanes, in the former age, that he will neither sing nor ' say something ', and only consents at last to give a bit of recitative from Euripides, the latest cry. When we leave the family and turn to the streets and public life our ears are dinned with the hubbub of perpetual litigation, the clamour of gossips, and the ceaseless chatter of the loungers in the Portico (the Paul's Walk of Athens), the gymnasiums, the baths, the barbers' and perfumers', or by the bankers' tables —any place where there were people to talk to and news to be heard.   The Gross Man (βδελυρός) is the sort of person who explains, as he stands at the door of the perfumer's, that he means to get drunk that night.   There is a great air, too, of petty business, of hard bargaining and harder crediting.   They seem to have carried ready-reckoners, as our ancestors did before the multiplication-table came in.   (Pepys, you may remember, got up at six in the morning to take lessons in it, being then a man of thirty and an important official at the Treasury.)   Lastly, there is a rousing atmosphere of street fraud, over which Theophrastian Athens and Elizabethan London may shake hands.   Greek drama, we know, was religious. Perhaps that is why these fourth-century Athenians took such pleasure in puppet-shows and conjurers' performances.   When the new moon came, Athens had a sort of Bartholomew Fair at which conjurers swallowed swords, drew pebbles from the ears of astonished spectators, and sang the latest songs. The Late-learner, in his effort to be up to date, goes time after time to try and get the songs by heart. They had even cock-fighting, these Athenians, and gambling-dens, and swarms of a class of men from whom we are mercifully spared, professional sooth-sayers. The Athenians were dreadfully superstitious. A mouse couldn't gnaw through a mealbag without sending the housewife to consult the wise man. Nowadays—such a thing is progress!—her husband would write to the *Weekly Postbag*, and all would be well. To end more sweetly and on the note of youth, they had lovers who serenaded. It is one of the symptoms of the Unseasonable Man that he will be such an ass as to serenade his mistress when she has a fever.

Such, then, is the society which Theophrastus has described in the clearest sketches of private life which Greek antiquity has left. It is surprising that the modern age, with its passion for *genre* and the realities of living, should have had so little to say all this while about Theophrastus. His book is short and his manner so unassuming that even the most pro-nounced of the moderns might find themselves very cosily at home with him in Athens. One great chance was missed when Robert Louis Stevenson, that 'better realist', turned a deaf ear to his friend John Symonds. They were at Davos together, and Stevenson was finishing *Treasure Island*. 'John Addington Symonds (to whom I timidly mentioned what I was engaged on) looked on me askance. He was at that time very eager I should write on the Characters of Theophrastus : so far out may be the judgements of the wisest men.' Was he, then, so very far out? Stevenson was right, of course, about *Treasure Island*; nothing could be allowed to interfere with that ; *hoc opus, hic labor*; but why should not he have written both? One breath of the homely Theophrastian air, so like the air of his own Scottish society, and he would have needed no second urging. An essay on the *Characters* by the panegyrist of 'a' the bonny U.P. Kirks' is a thing to think of. It would have been the finest thing in his pack.

The history of the *Characters*, on which we are now to enter, is for the greater part of it a history of form. It has two stages. The first is part of the history of the schools, the second is part of the history of mimicry, or of the comic spirit in man. As a rule, we hear only of this second stage ; historians of literature are in the habit of bringing in the Character with Casaubon's edition and translation at the end of the sixteenth century ; but the first was much longer, extending from Theophrastus's own day to the decline of the schools of rhetoric in the West. This double history of the book is a practical consequence of the circumstances in which it was composed. Theophrastus, when he wrote it, wrote in two qualities, as the contemporary of Menander and the successor of Aristotle. Writing with pleasure as an observer of his neighbours, he did not forget that he was also a professor, that though the spirit of Comedy might be the inspiration of the Character, Ethics was its basis and Rhetoric its end. The professor was taken at his word. The *Characters* were accepted as a model collection of ἤθη for the student, and their *milieu* became henceforth the *milieu* of the classroom in which they had first been read. They seem to have become popular at once, and to have retained their popularity throughout antiquity; were often imitated, and not only by Peripatetics : when Philodemus the Epicurean wrote his tenth book *De Vitiis* in Ciceronian Rome he had the *Characters* of Theophrastus before him.[1] But chiefly the book flourished in epitomes. The schoolmasters and teachers of rhetoric got hold of it, and drilled it into use ; it was such an excellent way of giving the young orator some idea of life before he had begun to live. Thus disguised, it passed to its place in the mediaeval curriculum, flourishing chiefly in the Eastern Empire, like all things Greek, but already embodied in the text-books of rhetoric which Rome bequeathed to her barbarians. By this route, and not, as is commonly supposed, in the train of Casaubon, the Character as a form of writing first reached England. It was called *Descriptio*,[2] and was set out in such manner as follows :

[1] The chief imitations are collected in Ussing's ed. (1868).

[2] The term is Cicero's : 'descriptio, quam Graeci χαρακτῆρα vocant' (*Top.* 22. 83). Another term was Notatio (*Rhet. ad Herenn.* iv. 50. 63). Casaubon hesitated which to choose for his title, but decided on Descriptio. Quintilian speaks of 'illa in scholis ἤθη' (vi. 2. 17).

Description of a mans nature or maners.

We describe the maners of men, when we set them
Descriptio forth in their kinde what they are. As in
speaking against a couetous man, thus. There is
no such pinch peney on liue as this good fellowe is.
He will not lose the paring of his nailes. His haire
is neuer rounded for sparing of money, one paire of
shone serueth him a twelue moneth, he is shod with
nailes like a Horse. He hath bene knowne by his
coate this thirtie Winter. He spent once a groate
at a good ale, being forced through companie, and
taken short at his worde, whereupon he hath taken
such conceipt since that time, that it hath almost
cost him his life.[1]

Now this is not only Theophrastian ; it is more
truly Theophrastian than the professed imitations
of Theophrastus ; yet it comes in mid-century in a
popular handbook of rhetoric, written and published
before Casaubon or Hall was born. There is only
one conclusion : it is that the Character was practised
in England before the *Characters* were known.
The first stage of their history, through whatever
disguises of epitome and tradition, had prepared the
way for the second. When, at the end of the sixteenth
century, they resumed their place as a substantive
work and exacted once more the public acknowledgements of imitators, their form and method was

---

[1] Wilson's *Arte of Rhetorique* (1553, 1560, &c.) : Clarendon Press
reprint, p. 187. The air of the proverb which hangs about this Character
is in the tradition. Proverbs, like Characters, were part of the young
orator's ammunition, and Theophrastus is said to have written a book on
Proverbs. The association of the Character and the Proverb was revived
by La Bruyère, who justified his maxims by pointing to Theophrastus's
lost treatise and the Proverbs of Solomon.

already familiar in the schools. It is curious to observe how completely this history carries out the immediate intention of their author. Epitomes apart, even the manuscript tradition of the *Characters* is almost wholly rhetorical. It was not until their scholastic intention was forgotten that the contemporary of Menander triumphed over the professor and claimed his reward once more as a spectator of men.

The date of this event is beyond dispute. It was the Latin version and commentary of Casaubon (1592) that first succeeded in restoring the author of the *Characters*, after all these centuries, to the quality of man of letters. His reasons for editing the book were various : because it was difficult, because its text was uncertain, and because he thought it instructive, as it is. Anything that is amusing and true cannot fail to be instructive. He lectured on it in the depressing college at Geneva under the shadow of Calvin and Beza, where it was perhaps just as well to say that you thought a thing instructive even if you found it amusing. He was a great scholar and an unsparing worker. Some of you may have read Mark Pattison's pitiless record of his life, with its cry of Time, Time, more Time— Theophrastus's cry. He grew ill, and his friends became alarmed. They took him from his books— he was in England the last four years of his life— and carried him to Greenwich for a change. ' I am like Theophrastus,' he said, ' dying of a holiday. When Theophrastus had passed his hundredth year, he went to his nephew's wedding, and gave up a day's study to do it. But he never studied more, he died of it.' Casaubon died three weeks later, on July 12, 1614. His *Theophrastus* was already in its third edition, and the interest, obvious everywhere, is most obvious in England. In 1610 John Healey left behind him the first translation of the *Characters* into English (it was published in 1616); in 1608, six years before Casaubon's death, appeared Joseph Hall's *Characters of Vertues and Vices*, the first professed imitation of Theophrastus in England. ' I have heere done it as I could,' says their author,

following that ancient Master of Moralitie, who thought this the fittest taske for the ninetie and ninth yeere of his age, and the profitablest monument that he could leave for a fare-well to his Grecians.

The Character, already familiar as a rhetorical form, was re-established in England as a definite gift of the ancient to the modern world, and when it entered on its hundred years of popularity, carried on it, definitely stamped, the name of Theophrastus.

Let us accept for a moment this genealogy of the Character in England and consider its history. The thing became a craze, more fashionable than sonnets. When Sir Thomas Overbury's posthumous collection appeared, in 1614, — ' Many witty Characters, and conceited Newes, written by himselfe and other learned Gentlemen his friends,'—it ran through five editions in the first year, and having begun with twenty-one Characters, finished up with eighty. It became, in fact, a miscellany of the most popular form of gentlemanly light literature of the time. From the tone of the character of ' An Elder

Brother' in the collection, and from other signs of wear and tear, I should judge that most of the contributors were younger sons. They have easier attitudes than Hall; they are amateurs, and have the air of the town. Their day, and how little it was likely to improve their fortunes, may be guessed from their manner of commending 'An Excellent Actor': 'He entertaines us in the leasure of our life, that is betweene meales, the most unfit time either for studie or bodily exercise.' After this collection, the most popular book of Characters was the *Microcosmographie* of John Earle, which was published anonymously in 1628 to forestall piracy, and was in its fifth edition in the following year. It is the best of these early collections, and perhaps of all the collections of Characters in English. As the century advanced, this sport, like every other, grew factious. The Character passed from the atmosphere of courts and studies to the busy offices of the pamphleteer, and at last to the garrets of literature, flourishing mightily in Pickthatch and in the neighbourhood of debtors' prisons. Hall, now a fighting Bishop, was privileged to see the form to which he had stood sponsor a generation ago drudging by his side. For all that it was a poor instrument of war. To put one's enemies into hell in generic terms is a game for the suburbs, and to do more, to name them, as some did, was to desert the principle of the style. Cleveland and Butler, of the later masters of the Character, kept its head high with their fantastic wit, but it sank steadily and disappeared at last in moral admonition in the works of William Law. Its bounds had long been broken, and its origin forgotten, so that you might have a Character of anything—of a Coffee-house, of Christmas, of France, of the World. The Character, in short, collapsed, because in an age of literary and civil confusion it was asked to do in its six inches of print what is now done by the essay, the leader, and the novel.

The place of Theophrastus in this movement is difficult to define. The only English Character-writer, so far as I know, who professes discipleship to Theophrastus is Hall, and it is possible that this profession has dissembled the genealogy. For though most of the writers of Characters must have read Hall, few besides Earle seem to have read Theophrastus. The ideal of the English Character—and we can see at once how much and how little of Theophrastus there is in it—is given in the collection of Overbury. 'To square out a Character by our English levell,' says the writer,

it is a picture (reall or personall) quaintly drawne, in various colours, all of them heightned by one shadowing. It is a quicke and soft touch of many strings, all shutting up in one musicall cloze : It is wits descant on any plaine song.[1]

Hall's chief contribution to this descant of wit was rhetoric ; and his models, the *Characters* of Theophrastus and his own sermons. From the first he learned perspective and compression, from the second a certain fervour of metaphor and peroration which the Character in England never

---

[1] *What a Character is* (ed. 1622 : Q4).

lost : the wit of likeness and allusion, and 'the tink in the close'. In his choice of subjects, also, he is liker Theophrastus than almost any of his successors, who thought more of the trades and occupations of men than of their generic qualities, describing with equal gusto a Hypocrite or an Hostler, a Milkmaid or a Bowling Alley, a Buttonmaker of Amsterdam or a Drunken Dutchman Resident in England. Hall's portraits are of virtues and vices simply, eleven of each, and it is noticeable that his vices are the better reading. Virtue being *ex hypothesi* the Mean, and the Mean being what society assumes, it is the divergences that are amusing. Hall's virtues read like fragments of his sermons, without the diffuseness that is permitted to that form of art ; and it is evident that he felt the disparity.

Perhaps in some of these (which thing I doe at once feare and hate) my stile shall seeme to some lesse grave, more Satyrical. . . . The fashions of some evils are besides the odiousnesse, ridiculous ; which to repeat, is to seeme bitterly merrie. I abhorre to make sport with wickednesse, and forbid any laughter heere, but of disdaine.[1]

It is a dilemma which never troubled Theophrastus. There is a great difference here from the Theophrastian manner. The quality of the laughter is different. To be bitterly merry, to refuse any laughter but of disdain, was to change the atmosphere in which Theophrastus wrote. The Ha! Ha! of seventeenth-century controversy is not the laughter of the social comedy. But it is one of the penalties of Christianity

[1] Book II : *Characterismes of Vices*, Proem.

which the world has agreed to prize that the more
we believe it to be true the less we are able to look
at society with a disinterested mind. The only man
of all these English writers who solved the problem
of being Christian and Theophrastian at once was
John Earle, because he was a quiet man in an age
of controversy, and read Theophrastus in the country.

This difference of faith is responsible for another
difference in method. Everything is pushed too far
back. Neither Hall nor his followers, in their descriptions of men, ever quite get away from the background of the First Parents and the Fall, which is
like doing geometry with the metaphysical problems
of space always in one's mind. No clear and neat
reasoning is possible. Euclid must be free to assume
space as he sees it ; let the metaphysician settle what
it is. But Hall seems always to be crying in his
heart, 'O Lord ! what is man?', unable or unwilling
to see that he is all the while appealing to the wrong
court, and that with these ultimate questions of life
the Character as such has nothing to do. What
Sainte-Beuve said of the Characters of La Bruyère
and Christianity should be true of all : *Ils s'en
passent.*

Lastly, you may see in Hall in embryo that violence
of metaphor which became the prevailing style of
the Character in England. It appears in him only
in peroration, but it is already doomed to success.
Theophrastus had told us what men do ; the whole
endeavour of the English writers was soon to tell us
what men are like. It became an exercise in egotism,
how to nourish the sprouts of your brain at the expense

of your subject. Every other sentence (till you try it) looks like the seed of an essay, and in short they are such lovers of half-lights, they so dote on the deformities of imagery and mind, that we begin to suspect them of having been deformities themselves, on the principle of that personage in Fielding's play who was so fond of intrigue that he really thought he must have been the son of one. In this style the rhyme of the Precious Man is verified, that

> Nothing is so retrograde
> As to call a spade a spade.

They shrink from the proximity of plain statement as from a precipice. Their writing motto is *ex ungue leonem*, and when they would paint a character, their method is a reversed *chiaroscuro* : given the shades, you are asked to find the lights. It is an orgy of allusion. The character of 'A Roaring Boy' is laid before us with the assurance that 'Don Quixote's water-mills are still Scotch bag-pipes to him'. They even brag of their obscurity, like the false prophets. 'Read what you list,' says Nicholas Breton, 'and understand what you can : Characters are not every man's construction, though they be writ in our mother tongue.'[1] This is cold comfort for the laity, who might have searched for merits and found them had they been less bluntly encouraged. The great merit of the English Characters was that no man could write in that style who had not read and reflected. Some of the finest wit in the language is imbedded in them—stunted and fruitless because of the form.

---

[1] *Characters upon Essaies* (1615) : To the Reader.

It is sometimes said that this form was such an excellent discipline for our Englishmen; that it taught them brevity, concentration, point. That it taught them some of these things is certain, and that Hall and Theophrastus have their share of credit for it; but it is a refinement of cruelty to applaud the discipline. When the law decides that a large man shall be confined in a small room it does not dwell on the consequence that he will be made neater in his movements. What the Character-writers were dying for was a new form to write in. They wanted to be stretched on print; something every day, no hoarding, and to go tired to bed. They wanted the essay, the leader, and the novel. If the Character could have stopped with Earle it would have been a blessing for many, for when Earle had done there was nothing left for it to do. The first Character in his book is the most poetical of all the English Characters, and I will end this analysis by quoting it:

A Child

Is a man in a small letter, yet the best copy of Adam before he tasted of Eve, or the apple; and he is happy whose small practice in the world can only write this character. He is nature's fresh picture newly drawn in oil, which time, and much handling, dims and defaces. His soul is yet a white paper unscribbled with observations of the world, wherewith at length it becomes a blurred note-book. He is purely happy, because he knows no evil, nor hath made means by sin to be acquainted with misery. He arrives not at the mischief of being wise, nor endures evils to come, by foreseeing them. He kisses and loves all, and when the smart of the rod is past, smiles on his beater. Nature and his parents alike dandle him, and tice him on with a bait of sugar to a draught of wormwood. He plays yet like a young prentice the first day, and is not come to his task of melancholy. His hardest labour is his tongue, as if he were loath to use so deceitful an organ; and he is best company with it when he can but prattle. We laugh at his foolish sports, but his game is our earnest: and his drums, rattles and hobby-horses, but the emblems, and mocking of man's business. His father hath writ him as his own little story, wherein he reads those days of his life that he cannot remember; and sighs to see what innocence he has out-lived. The elder he grows, he is a stair lower from God; and like his first father much worse in his breeches. He is the Christian's example, and the old man's relapse: the one imitates his pureness, and the other falls into his simplicity. Could he put off his body with his little coat, he had got eternity without a burden, and exchanged but one heaven for another.

I wish that we could rest in the easy genealogy of Hall's preface, which gives the Character in England one founder and one model; but it is evident that we cannot. It is too simple, and the record of divergence is too great. And in any case I should find it difficult to be content with a history of the Character which said nothing of Comedy, its companion and preceptor, or of the social Ethics which is at the root of both. More interesting even than the debt of Hall to Theophrastus, of Overbury to Hall, and of Earle to all three, is the debt of the

English Character to the English Comedy of Humours. It is a debt not confined to inspiration and precept, though it furnished both. The first examples, even, of the typical English Character are to be found not in Hall, but in Ben Jonson, in the sketches prefixed to *Every Man out of his Humor* (1600), and in the full-dress portraits in *Cynthia's Revels* (1601). Shift and Fastidious Brisk, in the first series, might stand among the Characters of Overbury without detection, and it is evident that they were not given casually. They are part of a scheme, specimens or first drafts from the note-book of 'the humorous poet', who chose this play in which to expound the whole philosophy of humours—the physical psychology of the age—and his intention to reform comedy by making a scenic science of them. His design was 'man', and an image of the times without romance or remorse.

> Well I will scourge those apes,
> And to these courteous eies oppose a mirror
> As large as is the Stage whereon we act,
> Where they shall see the times deformity,
> Anatomiz'd in euery Nerue and sinew,
> With constant courage, and contempt of feare.[1]

I know no passage which better describes the aim and temper of the Comedy of Humours, or, let me add, of the typical English Character. 'Deformities' is the word in both; and 'Anatomy' was a synonym for Character. Cleveland, writing in 1647, uses the language of Jonson : 'Every Char-

---

[1] *Every Man out of his Humor*, Induct.

acter', he says, 'is an anatomy lecture.'[1]   It is the
difference between the English and the Theophrastian Character in six words.

In *Cynthia's Revels* Jonson brought matters to
a head.   The analyses in this play are a deliberate
advance on the prefatory sketches of the previous
year.   They are promoted from the frontispiece to
the text.   A dozen characters or so, of masking vices,
are passed in review, and their anatomy achieved in
set terms by the manager of the piece.   Seven are
analysed at length : Hedon, or the Man of Pleasure ;
Anaides, or the Shameless Gallant ; Amorphus, the
Affected Traveller, and his understudy, Asotus ; and
three ladies.   The chief showman in this menagerie
of humours is Mercury, and there are varieties.   We
are admitted to a physiognomical lecture on faces
by one of the menagerie, Amorphus, who also obliges
with a very pretty analysis of himself, not as others
saw him.   At the end, when the virtues come in,
their counterfeits are exposed and sentenced by
Arete and Crites, the true critic—Jonson's *honnête
homme* or 'man of sense'.   It is an Aristotelian-
Theophrastian lecture put upon the stage, with
Virtue and the Mean for expositor and judge!
In a later addition to the play one of the ladies as
good as asks for a Book of Characters.   Phantaste
would have lovers 'of all humours', she says, 'and
of all complexions', and see how love works 'in a
cholericke man, and a sanguine ; in a melancholique,
and a phlegmatique ; in a foole and a wise man ; in
a clowne and a courtier'.   'And then', she goes on,

The Character of a Diurnal-maker.

I to haue a booke made of all this, which I would call the booke of humours, and euery night reade a little piece, ere I slept, and laugh at it.[1]

When we reckon that from about this date to the end of the century nearly two hundred such Books of Humours issued from the press, we see not only that Phantaste was voluminously answered but that she did not wish at random. Judge from this specimen how far Ben Jonson approved of her wish and had all along the means of supplying it. It is the Character of the Affected Traveller, Ulysses-Politropus-Amorphus—for such and no less was his name—and it is Mercury who speaks.

He that is with him, is Amorphus, a trauailer, one so made out of the mixture and shreds of formes, that himselfe is truly deform'd. He walkes most commonly with a cloue, or pick-tooth in his mouth, hee is the very mint of complement, all his behauiours are printed, his face is another volume of *essayes* ; and his beard is an *Aristarchus*. He speakes all creame, skimd, and more affected then a dozen of waiting women. He is his owne promoter in euery place. The wife of the ordinarie giues him his diet, to maintaine her table in discourse, which (indeed) is a meere tyrannie over her other guests, for hee will usurp all the talk : ten constables are not so tedious. He is no great shifter, once a yeere his apparell is readie to reuolt. He doth use much to arbitrate quarrels, and fights himselfe, exceeding well (out at a window). He will lye cheaper then any begger, and lowder than most clockes : for which he is right properly accommodated to the *whetstone*, his page.[2]

---

[1] *Cynthia's Revels*, IV. i (Folio, 1616).   [2] *Ibid*. II. iii.

The play in which this Character appears was acted in 1600 and published in 1601, seven years before the *Characters* of Hall, and we are faced with a dilemma. Was Jonson a Theophrastian, like Hall? If he was, then his are the first full-drawn Theophrastian Characters in English, and Theophrastus has added a greater name than any to the list of his imitators. If he was not, we must adjust the accepted pedigree of the Character in England; Theophrastus is no longer the first model of the English Character, and Hall's examples are a modifying accident after the event. I am inclined to believe that Jonson was not a Theophrastian, though he knew the *Characters* and occasionally borrows from them.[1] Had he been consciously indebted to Theophrastus for the idea of the Character he must have cited him among his masters in some one or other of the numerous stage-lectures on *Quid sit comoedia?* by which he chose to instruct the public at the expense of his plays. The English Character, I conclude, is in the main a by-product of the Comedy of Humours, accidentally determined, at an early moment in its history, by the opportune appearance of Theophrastus's model. Of these two strains in the Character, the Theophrastian and Jonsonian, the first is most apparent in Hall, and the second, as we should expect from their life about town, in the work of Overbury and his friends. As for

---

[1] Cp. *Volpone*, iv. 1: 'A rat had gnawne my spurre-lethers,' &c., with *Theophr. Char.* xvi: καὶ τὴν ὁδὸν ἐὰν ὑπερδράμῃ γαλῆ, κτλ. Mr. Percy Simpson, who directed me to this parallel, assures me that ' such borrowings from Theophrastus in Jonson are rare '.

Jonson,—something, no doubt, he learned, like others, from the rhetorical tradition of the Character, from Casaubon's version, and from such sketches of street types as Harman's and Greene's, but on the whole the Jonsonian comedy would seem to be a grafting of the scientific theory of humours on the social portraiture of Plautus and Terence, the Roman descendants of Menander, and to be new chiefly because of the exaggerated resolution with which the experiment was carried out. In the business of anatomy to which his theory led him he would forget that, while Galen was busy, Plautus and Terence were standing still.

Pro. Well, *Boy*, it is a fair Presentment of your *Actors*; and a handsome promise of somewhat to come hereafter.

Dam. But there is nothing done in it, or concluded: Therefore I say, no Act.

Boy. A fine piece of Logick![1]

The world, I believe, has always sympathized with Mr. Damplay, and refused to be put down by the Boy. Jonson was the first man in England to produce the set Character on scientific principles, and he deserves all the credit it may bring him, for he spoilt most of his comedies to do it.

I believe that this relation of the Character to Comedy is normal, and that wherever the Character appears it will be found to be somehow an abstract from Comedy, made in the interest of the social Ethics which is at the root of both. In the struggle to present the images of common life it is always the theatre which first reaches perfection,

---

[1] *The Magnetick Lady; or, Humors Reconcil'd*, Act i, Chorus.

and the set Character is the stage Character in still
life. The comic spirit of Theophrastus's *Characters*
has been recognized by scholars—*mimicum genus,
festivum genus scribendi*—and the best commentary
on them is that which draws most fully from the
Middle and New Comedy of Athens, which points
from his Δεισιδαίμων and Ἀλαζών to Menander's, and
from his Ὀψιμαθής to the Old Man, *Senex*, of Attic and
Roman Comedy,—as you may see him still, after all
those years, in the terra-cotta from Myrina, dancing
and kissing his hands. When we turn to England,
to the crowded scenes of Jonson and the rabble of
Characters, there is the same congruity. The Courtier
walking in Paul's 'with a pick-tooth in his hat'; the
Pert Lady with her 'neat youth'; the Affected
Traveller with his shrugs, his oaths, and his boy; the
round-breeched Puritan, challenging the Almighty
daily to talk with him extempore; the Inns of Court
Man, with his silk stockings, his beaver hat, and his
contempt of study; the Fine Gentleman who wears
pumps in his pocket 'lest fiddlers should take him
unprovided'; the Mere Fellow of a College, 'respect-
ing no man within the University and respected by
no man out of it'; the quack physician, the astrologer,
the alchemist—you may study them all indifferently
in the Characters or in Ben Jonson, for in their
picture of Vanity Fair the Book of Characters and
the Book of Humours are at one. The character-
writer most conscious of this relation was La Bruyère.
In that part of his book where he criticizes authors
(*Des Ouvrages de l'Esprit*) he praises Molière like
a rival. Molière has too strong a brush for La

Bruyère. If only he had been more Terentian! Or rather, if Molière and Terence could have been combined, 'Quel homme on aurait pu faire de ces deux comiques!' We know this type of praise. If only Shakespeare had been more Jonsonian! La Bruyère will not submit whole-heartedly even to Alceste and Tartuffe. The true misanthrope, we discover, is liker his own Timon, the true hypocrite liker his own Onuphre. He had the analyst's impatience of invention, and shrank from that alliance of stage and study which Steele and Addison so welcomed even to the length of censuring the comic theatre altogether. It is the clearest case of 'two of a trade'. He felt that here also he had come, as he said, 'too late.' The master of French comedy was dead fifteen years before his book appeared.

It is the last stage in the history of the Character, and contains the moral of the whole. We had been writing Characters for three-quarters of a century when La Bruyère published his *Caractères* in 1688, and took Paris by storm. His scheme was tentative. He began with a translation of Theophrastus, and the addition, as by after-thought, of some characters of his own ; but the success of the book overcame his reticence. His contributions grew with each edition until the translation became in appearance what it had perhaps always been in reality, an occasion merely and starting-point for his own excursions. We may learn from his exuberant praise of Theophrastus what trust to put in prefaces. Owing little to Theophrastus but the bare idea, and everything that a writer so original could owe to the

writers of his own country, he makes no mention of
Montaigne among his masters, talks, as I have said,
of Molière with the clouded face of a rival, and when
he remembers his obligations to Pascal and La
Rochefoucauld is only concerned to explain that he
was not their pupil. It is the old game which our
ancestors played every day : the authors of antiquity
being outside the range of rivalry, when you are
indebted to a modern, praise an ancient. The
popularity of the *Caractères* was not confined to
France ; they were well known in England. Addison
knew them, and was influenced by them—how much, is
a question in which perhaps Englishmen will never
be interested, and on which Frenchmen will perhaps
always exaggerate. The two men are curiously
alike. Though La Bruyère had passed current in
society all his life, yet no one seems to have known
him or to have been able to say more of him than
this, that he was *un fort honnête homme.* Put these
words into English, and what more do we know of
Addison ? These were the men for whom the
Character had been waiting ; the man for the
Theophrastian task should be himself the Mean. It
was perhaps by no accident that they should both
have assisted in a second Theophrastian revival ; that
as La Bruyère translated Theophrastus in 1688,
Addison should have recommended, and been sus-
pected of having revised and even written the translation of Theophrastus which his nephew Eustace
Budgell published in 1714. Both men were aware,
before or after, that in their advance from set
characters, portraits, and maxims to the essay, they

were carrying a task to its conclusion. Theophrastus had told us what men do; Hall and his successors what men are like; it was left for these two writers to tell society in essays what men are. Almost from the first the Character had been somehow aware of the Essay, and of its destiny there. You may see it in some of the spurious epilogues in Theophrastus; in the 'Essay of Valour' among the Characters of Overbury; and in the constant title of the English collections, 'Essaies or Characters.' If Nicholas Breton is to be believed, the Essays of Bacon were as congenial to the English character-writers as Montaigne was to La Bruyère.[1]

The destiny of the Character in the Essay was not achieved, however, without a struggle, even by its latest practitioners. Some fate seemed to have determined that we should do all over again in this matter what Plutarch had done long ago in Greece: for Plutarch's discourses 'Of Garrulity', 'Of Curiosity', and the like, are Characters turned Essays, or they are nothing. He is to Theophrastus in antiquity what Addison is to Earle, and it is no small part of the secret of Montaigne that he alone of the early essayists had the instinct to enter directly into the labours of Plutarch, saving himself thereby a whole century of trouble in the fusing of forms. In this necessary fusion La Bruyère was never quite successful, and Addison and Steele had as

[1] 'Worthy Knight, I have read of many Essaies, and a kinde of Charactering of them, by such, as when I lookt into the forme, or nature of their writing, I have beene of the conceit, that they were but Imitators of your breaking the ice to their inventions.'—*Characters upon Essaies*, 1615: Dedication to Sir Francis Bacon.

many failures as successes. In many of the essays
in the *Tatler* and *Spectator* you may see the Character
in both styles, French and English, standing disengaged as in a portrait. The character of the
dévote might have been written by La Bruyère, and
Tom Folio, with the change of a word or two, might
take his place in the *Microcosmographie* of Earle.[1]
It was the misfortune of La Bruyère that he could
never forget his predecessors. He came at the end
of a long and restless line, and felt it; Addison at the
beginning of something new, and felt it also. Man
was still in disgrace in the seventeenth century; it was
the good fortune of Addison to feel the first stirrings
of his restoration. Writing with a confidence and
repose denied to La Bruyère he achieved the essay,
and in his happier moments reached the novel. His
annoyance at Steele for meddling with Sir Roger is
the feeling of a novelist for his creation.

There is only one thing more that I should like to
say, by way of epilogue. It touches, I believe, the
root of Character-making. All these Characters
should imply a normal type of man, a standard of
some sort for our imitation. In Athens he is the
μεγαλόψυχος, the Magnanimous Man; in France he is
l'honnête homme; in Addison's England he is whatever
is the English for *l'honnête homme*, the man of sense,
and in Jonson's, the man of balance. Now, whatever we may think of the social value of these types,
it is evident that not one of them is a type of man

[1] *Spectator*, No. 354; *Tatler*, No. 158 (para. 1).

at his best. The whole notion of the Mean is in fact
a burgess notion, condemned by its very principle to
stare for life at the heroisms and excesses for which
it can make no provision. It is the enemy of all
raptures, driving the Puritan to his Synod and the
Artist to his Bohemia, and every Renaissance is
a revolt against it. I should like to know what
a Greek of the age of Pericles would have thought
of that line in *Hamlet*,

Cut off even in the blossoms of his sins.

Alcibiades and his friends would have understood it ;
he is one of the Renaissance figures of antiquity, and
suffered for it. Society could not use him, and he
became a thing only to be wondered at. Pericles
had hit the perfect note, 'Beauty without expense,'
and the moderate man cheered a compromise. But
Beauty at any cost is the Renaissance ideal. I
suppose we must go on submitting to the Mean, if
only for the sake of each other ; there is this comfort
that it always goes at a crisis. Consider the heavy-
footed μεγαλόψυχος, or *l'honnête homme*, how different
they are from our idea of the Athenians or the
French. The reason is that we have taken our idea
of these nations from their behaviour at a crisis.
Our idea is the right one. The other is only protective colouring. Look within our own island, even :
there is no more restless, passionate, or loquacious
people than the Scots, and yet they have actually
imposed on the world their protective ideal of the
'canny'! To a spirited people the Mean can seldom
be more than a business subterfuge.

THE GREEK ROMANCES

By J. S. PHILLIMORE

THERE are so few parts of literature in which the Greeks did not excel, that it is not unreasonable to approach the study of the Novel by stating the question thus : 'How comes it that this great province of art was mainly left for modern develop-ment?' One part of the answer which I shall attempt to justify in these pages will sound at first blush like a paradox. The Greeks failed here, in so far as they did fail, and for so long, for want of free individual initiative in invention. This is a fault which makes the counterpart to their greatest quality : their finest work was habitually didactic in purpose, traditional in form, collective in inspiration. Their greatest authors, supreme masters in many forms, yet only develop by cautious modification the instru-ments which unconscious collective or national invention has struck out in the rough. He that best administers is the best craftsman. The origins of their greatest forms—the Epic, the Tragedy, the Comedy—are lost in the mists of antiquity, to which the fumes of modern controversy only add further darkness. It is typical that an Asclepiadean or a Phalaecian metre bears the name, not of its inventor,

but of the poet who employed it most familiarly and
with most mastery.

The very form of our inquiry puts one in mind of
that famous chapter in which a Roman critic, writing
in the maturity of Latin culture, strikes a balance of
achievement between the two literatures. Quintilian's oft-quoted sentence allows the Romans a clear
superiority over the Greeks in only one form of
literature, the *Satira*, the invention of Menippus, a
half-Semite, and a thing so irregular and free and
subjective that it was forbidden to the Greeks by
that instinct which led them in all the greater exhibi-
tions of their art completely to suppress the author
in the creation, the actor in the part played. For
their great principle, expressed in the very term
μίμησις, insists on the mask and the make-believe ;
but in the *Satira* the poet speaks on his own authority ; his value as a man determines the value of his
words : even a Horace, with all his irony, speaks as
a bard or a seer. It was not so in the noblest
masterpieces of Greek : there the poet goes for
almost nothing : his poem is impersonally put on
trial, to stand its chance by the less or more of
beauty and consistency in it. Most notably of all,
Homer and Sophocles keep doggedly behind the
scenes, denying themselves to all the calls of *Author !*
which many centuries of inquisitive spectators have
addressed to them. This belongs to the great and
lasting Greek 'convention of Dignity' : it is all of
a piece with that other rule—that only great public
personages are fit subjects for the central interest of
a serious piece.

So much for a first disability, manifest in the classical period : the stern custom of artistic dignity.

But on the other hand the talent for story-telling, ἔκθεσις πράγματος γεγονότος ἢ ὡς γεγονότος,[1] may be called the greatest and the most universal of the Greek endowments. As in their mythology, no imagination, lovely, quaint, frightful, or obscene, that ever crossed the most visionary, the most grotesque, the most morbid, the most perverse moods of the brain, but was embodied for ever in the symbol of a myth ; so in their literature, from the very beginnings of Epic, there is such mastery in the art of telling a story, as would alone be enough to convict anybody who might be deluded into taking the Homeric poems for the primitive woodnotes of unsophisticated genius. Not less in the αἶνος of Hesiod, and even more plainly in the narrative monologue of a Tragedy, can we see this same bent for playing in words the masque of something which has happened in action, or might have happened. How Aeschylus or Sophocles revels and luxuriates when he has a story to tell in the third person ; a scene to re-create in words ; nay, even more interesting, a character to invent freely for once, untutored by traditional legend and the convention of dignity—a Watchman, or a Nurse, or a Messenger!

Nor is it only in poetry. We need not doubt that when in later ages we find the teachers of style so strong on the importance of this narrative part in a speech, that they are carrying on the tradition which those much-abused first Professors of Literature, the Sicilian sophists, had formulated. There

[1] Nicolaus Soph. Progymn. (Spengel, ii, p. 450).

is this much truth in the concluding sentence of an interesting book which is full of hazardous assertions, Reitzenstein's *Hellenistische Wundererzählungen.*

' Nobody can be the historian of the Romance or the Elegy who has not followed up the clues of the rhetorical curriculum and the aesthetic theory of the Hellenistic period.'

Gorgias and the other Intellectuals (σοφισταί) who trained men to power and influence by improving them in the quality which outweighed all others in the esteem of that nation of dilettanti—eloquence— must needs pay great attention to this very important element in the success of a speech, the Narrative. Both the narrative of fact, told with an artful bias towards the pleader's side (εἰs τὸ ὑπὲρ τοῦ λέγοντος μέρος ῥέπουσα [1]), for lawyers ; and the free invention, the μῦθος or αἶνος, which should have allegorical force and be, like metaphor, a dissembling argument in the subtle medium of symbolism.

There is evidently no room for even the rudiments of the Novel, as we conceive it, until Prose becomes a professionally systematized art, and so far asserts itself against Poetry that a frontier must be delimited between them. This time came in the fifth century B.C. Poetry made some concessions, but the one thing needful here was not conceded. It still remained unquestioned that the sphere of pure imagination belonged to Poetry ; and Poetry means ' any piece of language in a given musical time ' (πάντα μέτρον ἔχοντα λόγον), as Gorgias excellently defined it, in terms which are prescriptive against

[1] Spengel, ii, p. 450.

a deal of modern nonsense. 'Creation,' ποίησις, implied this. 'Creation,' ποίησις, they knew; λόγος, 'talk,' they knew; they even admitted (under protest[1]) a new kind of man who 'wrote down talk', a λογο- γράφος; but he was not licensed to 'create' in the proper sense. A great battle was gained when (in the fourth century B.C.) Prose successfully challenged this privilege also; doubtless it was a victory which had been long preparing by the over-refinement, over-development, and dissipation of metre. When Poetry requires musical accompaniment to explain and justify it to the ear, Prose has an opportunity. We have here an eternal force in art, the law of *brevis in perfecto mora*. Forms die of perfection. When there are no secrets left for curiosity, no career for ambition, it is time for a *Ver Sacrum* of exploring invention. In Greek literature a certain vein was worked out after Euripides, as was the case after Ovid, and the case at the end of the eighteenth century in England.

We must reckon the death of Tragedy for a great epoch in the coming of the Novel. Though Tragedy died intestate, the New Comedy could claim as a somewhat remote next of kin; and it was Menander and those others to whom the New Comedy belongs, who inherited the sentimental *motifs* and the humanitarian fingering and fondling of the poignant but unheroic emotions which Euripides the disintegrator had brought into honour. The convention

---

[1] Alcidamas's protest is extant: it contains the interesting phrase, 'those who devote themselves entirely to writing their compositions ought to be called *poets* rather than *Intellectuals*.'

of dignity must be broken again. Only now, when the tyrannical grip of the petty Commonwealth was relaxed, was the individual allowed to discover and explore himself. The fortunes and the feelings not of kings and chieftains and prophets and heroines, not even of great generals and politicians, but of the ordinary bourgeois of Athens, were now to be the staple matter of drama. '*Comoedi sunt qui privatorum hominum acta dictis aut gestu cantabant.*' So we are one stage advanced, but a devious stage of a long journey. For Drama meant an Action, still far removed from λόγος, a talk. Dialogue is a means of Action, no doubt; but the most narrative part of the old drama, the ῥῆσις, now actually fell out; and nobody dreamed of such a revolution as a Drama of literary rank, written in prose.

Meanwhile another condition was coming into play. Once you destroy a State's political independence, you throw the individual back on his own single resources of emotion. How is he to amuse himself? There are two individual experiences, and only two, so significant that they make all else seem silly as a 'temperance' drink in comparison with wine: Religion and Love. The Greeks have never been passionately interested in Religion as the social expression of heroic goodwill, only as matter for the curious speculations of individual dilettanti. So the love *motif* becomes inevitably for them the only certain stimulus of excitement. And for those who understand by Romance something in which the love interest predominates, Greek literature is in mid-romance by the end of the fourth century B.C.

So the traditional obstacles keep breaking down
and the new forces gathering. The process advances
yet a step : but still Romance, though it be a presence,
is not a form.

In surveying the history of the Greek novel,
everything turns out so pat as it ought, that the
cautious critic who knows how reality rebels against
neat systems can hardly believe his eyes. And yet
it seems true. The Athenian remains characteris-
tically central, content with few forms, soberly
evolving; he evinces his supreme craftsmanship by
his facility for dealing in a received currency, true to
the great principle of artistic frugality ; here, as in
the type of his Attic idiom, able to make much
significance out of little stuff and little effort, without
meanness. For his φιλοκαλοῦμεν μετ' εὐτελείας is a law
of economy in craft as well as of finance.

The novelties which bridge old divisions and make
hybrid forms, and, ' in the luckiest event' (as the
Lottery circulars say), new and fertile species, must
come from abroad. It is provincials, in prise to
foreign civilizations, who innovate. Stesichorus,
whose greatness we can only calculate as astronomers
infer the presence of an undiscernible star, whose
work was by means of dramatic lyrics to prepare
Epic legend for tragic treatment—Stesichorus,
curiously enough, also reveals some of the first
sporadic hints of an inchoate Romanticism in his
Kalyke and *Rhadina*.[1] This is no more by chance

---

[1] Not extant.

than it is by chance that Euripides, far more deeply sophisticated by the great prose rhetoricians than Aeschylus or Sophocles, first largely admits the romantic and sentimental interest into Tragedy ; or that the first Athenian who writes what can properly be called a Prose romance at all is Xenophon, an *émigré*, in revolt against Atticism, made familiar with Asia (that half-hellenized background of Greek civilization) by his campaigns. In this child of the sophistic era, who is also a knight-errant and a bit of a village patriarch, Athens has *à la rigueur* its first novelist. From a strictly Attic point of view there was always something queer and incongruous about Xenophon : this freak might have been expected of him. But if we allow that there is a novel in the *Cyropaedia*, the novel is imperfectly disengaged : you can see yet sticking to it and obscuring its contours much that betrays how διήγησις in the sophist routine was not a self-subsistent whole, and anything like free invention was known only as a feature introduced for didactic ends : μῦθος εἰκονίζων τὴν ἀλήθειαν.[1] But it is only one step from Allegory to Romance, as Prudentius's *Psychomachia* proved to the Dark Ages. And though the *Cyropaedia* is little more than an expansion of the Fable as recommended for use in rhetoric, it is immensely nearer to a Novel than the Platonic Myth.

The point has been disputed whether the Novel owes anything to influences definitely un-Greek. There is no room for doubt. Xenophon and his like play the part of fertilizing insects. The Novel

[1] Spengel, ii, p. 453.

is an import. But why should it be held a humiliation for the Greeks to import raw material? The old boast that Greek art sprang by miracle fully armed from Athena's head has been rudely shaken by the unveiling of the backgrounds.

In any case, can we resist the induction which results from merely setting down the names of the earliest ascertained writers in whom an inchoate Romance is discernible? Stesichorus of Himera, Ctesias of Cnidos, Xenophon the adventurer, Timaeus[1] of Taormina. A meticulous analysis might discover traces in Herodotus of Halicarnassus. Add to these the veins of romantic legend embedded in the local histories of Ionian cities, especially the two which were never to lose their primacy in this kind—Ephesus and Miletus. What is the inference? That Romance is something which arises always on the borders of Hellenism, and often derives its themes from over the border, e. g. a Cyrus and a Dido.

And now with the disappearance of genius comes, as usual, the improvement of schooling : failing φυά (to put it in Pindaric terms), what can μάθησις do? It is the day of Professors and Lecturers, σοφισταί and ῥήτορες. From the fifth century onwards the teaching of style and literature was steadily developed and perfected. And as all the other parts in the curriculum were improved, so more particularly perhaps was the *Narrative* improved, because audiences had more and more taste for this. Any of the handbooks or treatises on Style will attest the fact, whether we look in Aristotle or in Cicero. There is usually an

---

[1] Timaeus was the first who used the theme of Aeneas and Dido.

' omnibus' literary form in any period.   At one time all the best stuff goes into Tragedy ; at another into Essays ; or again, into Novels.   This was the heyday of the Declaimed Essay.   And into speech or lecture form went also faculties that had once been employed in the drama.   Cicero says no more than a great truism when he says, following of course a Greek master, that applied Psychology is the essence of good oratory.   In fact, more and more of the components of literature were being brought into the net of the Professors of Style; they taught the art of story-telling and the art of analysing and displaying motives of character.   For a time there was room for everything in the Stylistic Exercise : but not for long.   The one form soon had more than it could carry : another periodic disintegration was due.   Let me take a simile from other arts.   Suppose the column, at first strictly designed for the support of a roof, and gradually in that employment more elaborated and ornamented : it will some day occur to some artist's fancy to excerpt this detail and make it an independent form, for— say—a pedestal.   Or again: after many old masters have painted the mountain, the stream, the little town, the flower-bed, in a background or as a mere accessory in composition, some one will anon take the notion of painting a landscape as such, or a flower study as such.   On the one hand fancy grows shortsighted, and shrinks to the appreciation of a smaller unit of beauty, more highly magnified ; on the other hand, the artist's scope of synthesis diminishes as his details are refined, and he condescends upon a particularized fraction of the former subject.

So in Greek Literature. Seen in retrospect, it is for us a strange case of arrested development that the humorous study of types in human character, so perfected in Theophrastus, could fail to produce the psychological novel there and then. But Theophrastus came too soon: before the New Comedy had effected its part of the release, by proving that mere bourgeois humanity as such was level with literature. And before that lesson could be applied, another disturbing influence had broken in—the outburst of Alexandrian poetry. Euphorion, Philetas, Callimachus, Theocritus, and Apollonius were all poets by instinct, and being all literary poets were true to the old doctrine that Verse was the proper medium for imaginative composition. There is no extremer example of this prejudice than the Mimes of Herodas; the mimic poems of Theocritus (ii, xiv, xv) are hardly less in point. Far from advancing any further, Prose seems rather to lose ground at this epoch: Apollonius's Medea also shows what a taking of psychology into Poetry there was just now—now at the very time when the Novel, the real Novel, was at last beginning to be written.

For there is no doubt that Alexandria produced novels. We have here the same conditions as in Ephesus or Miletus or Syracuse: a glaze of Greek on a block of foreign stuff which shows its colours and patterns through. But the novel of Alexandria was a popular, backstairs business; too vernacular in inspiration for the mandarins of literature to concern themselves with it : second-class literary matter like the street-corner sermons of Cynic and Stoic itinerants.   This chap-book or penny-novelette style of thing could not be admitted above the salt at the banquet of Letters.

As one pursues this inquiry, time and again one is put in mind of those lovers in Charito or Achilles Tatius or Heliodorus, whose happy meeting, apparently inevitable in the next chapter, is again deferred by the malignant freaks of Chance.   A winding road with many *faux coins de route !*   Here are all the elements apparently present : the psychology, the romantic interest, and even a new impulse in the Travellers' Tales which came thick and three-fold after Alexander had revealed the Far East : yet always some Fate seems to forbid the banns.   The Convention of Dignity was broken : yet no genius arose who was both willing and qualified to pass a spark through the awaiting elements.   The rhetoricians could not train a man to invent the great new synthesis.   And so the analysis of ethical types was still left with the philosophers; the display of them in dialogue still remained with Comedy and Mime, still addicted to Verse ; and the tender and passionate stories must still be told in metre by elegists and epyllionists.   ' If youth but knew ! If age but had the power !'

But it was something that the popular chap-book written by stuttering and bungling feuilletonists, for the unlearned, in a tongue which the Museum scorned, was come into being at all.   The reign of

Poetry was not to last for ever.   But till Poetry was silenced, or at least reduced to chirps of epigram, Prose fiction could not assert itself.   Nothing could force down the resistance of the classical dogma, and the prose novelist was powerless against the traditional sovereignty of verse till Poetry itself, in final decay, abdicated the imaginative province.   It is very significant that Parthenius of Nicaea, to whom we owe much of our information about the romantic themes of Mythology, drew up his little manual of ἐρω-τικὰ παθήματα for the express purpose of providing the poet Cornelius Gallus with materials for Latin elegies and epyllia.

We have seen that the rudiments of the Novel appeared here and there on the edge of the Greek world, where it fringed Persian, Egyptian, and Phoenician influences.   Another conclusion arises from the date and certain of the personalities with which the eventual rise of this pale and late-born star is connected. The first man to whom the title of Novelist can be given without reservation, meaning an admitted man of letters who wrote what would pass muster as a feuilleton in a newspaper, is one Antonius Diogenes, whom the learned patriarch Photius assigns to a date little after Alexander the Great.   But his bilingual name makes this incredible; it proclaims him for a Greek freedman or client of a Roman patron, a relation hardly conceivable before the First Punic War and not probable before the Second.   We may safely place him in the first century B.C.   The loss of this author's twenty-four books of *Strange Tales from beyond Thulé* need not cost us many tears.   It served Lucian as stuff for parody, and its vague, even monstrous, amorphism is recorded in Photius's summary.   Next consider that story which Plutarch tells: how after the defeat of Carrhae the Parthians were scandalized by finding in the baggage of a Roman officer of Crassus's army the pornographic novel known as *Milesian Tales*.   (We picture a virtuous Chinaman horrified at an English colonel's pocket Zola.) Aristides of Miletus was the author of this stuff, which seems to have pleased the somewhat crude Roman appetite.

We conclude then that the last and most decisive of the foreign impacts which made the Novel take shape is the impact of Greek on Roman.   Quintilian does not take credit for Petronius ; but had he chosen to advance the claim, what modern critic could have gainsaid him ?   Still more incontestable is Apuleius's superiority over any Greek rival.

We can see that the rhetoric schools at Athens or Rhodes must have become much more real and lively when they began to be peopled with Roman students who were going to make careers by their eloquence when they had got it trained: ῥητορική had not meant so much since Athens lost her independence.   And it may well be that the *Narratio* shared extra largely in a general renovation of all parts of the curriculum.   Rewards tell.   In England in Queen Anne's reign Latin verses were pretty well written, and excited real interest, because then you got a snug living out of the taxes for writing a nice copy of elegiacs.   Moreover, fresh students refresh a routine of teaching: they bring original points of

view, unspoiled curiosities, new ideas.   This much is
certain : nowhere can we so plainly see the affinity
between Novel and Rhetoric as in the *Controversiae*
of Seneca and those which go by Quintilian's name.
The theme set for declamation in debate is in many
cases a perfect nucleus for a Romance.   The stock
figures of Romance are there : amorous gallants,
lovely maidens, wicked stepmothers, cruel fathers,
the tyrant, the pirate, the outlandish brigands.
Pompey's campaign put the real pirates into the
region of bygones, long enough past to take on
romantic possibilities : so a name which has been
awfully significant in actual experience, still, as an
echo, vaguely thrills the imagination of posterity,
soon to end as a bogy, like the Spaniards, or Guy
Faux, or Napoleon.

Who knows but what it was not only the fresh curiosity of new students, but something in the Latin genius
itself, which convinced the *blasés* Greeks that this
bit of the school exercise was very interesting in itself
and might be specialized into a literary version of
those vulgar chap-books which the unlettered mobs
of Alexandria and Ephesus liked so well ?   Crassus's
officers at least prove a taste for one of the attributes
of the new kind of book, its lusciousness.   The part
of Sir Pandarus was one to which the Graeculus lent
himself kindly and aptly.

However this may be, Greek Poetry being now so
long silent as to be presumed dead, when Invention
at last looked about seriously for a comfort to her
widowed state, her choice of a young branch of the
Rhetoric business, now setting up on his own, was

highly approved and promoted by Roman taste.
And out of deference to his predecessor in the
marriage, Number Two starts with a devout resolve
to imitate his qualities as far as may be, by great
attention to verbal beauties, and to rhythm, assonance,
and all that equipment which Greek Poetry had
systematized to death.

The especial form of Poetry which the Novel con-
tinues, transformed, is undoubtedly the Alexandrian
Elegy: Elegy in chief, Epyllion and Pastoral to
a less degree. But, in a way, as we have seen, it
became also representative of Drama; for Photius's
sentence is true, '*There are two morals in all this
fiction and extravagance: wickedness eventually
punished, and the innocent marvellously saved after
many hair's-breadth escapes.*' This, in the eyes of the
Byzantines, was enough to excuse the conventional
sensuousness of the Novel. The artists in the new
medium are significantly known as ἐρωτικοί, and their
work collectively as ἐρωτικά. But Photius calls both
Iamblichus's lost romance and Diogenes Antonius's
δραματικόν; Eustathius's Byzantine imitation he calls
δρᾶμα outright. Clitophon in Achilles Tatius (A. 9. 1)
calls his experiences τὸ δρᾶμά μου. The individual
titles are sometimes attached to a certain place, like
the *Babyloniaca* of Iamblichus and the alternative
sub-title of *Aethiopica* for Heliodorus's book: more
usually, they bear the names of the lovers whose
passionate pilgrimages are told: as, *The Tale of
Theagenes and Chariclea*, or of *Chaereas and Callirrhoe*, or of *Leucippe and Clitophon*.

Prescinding from the Alexander-Romance, which is a separate thing, and would quite burst the frames of an already crowded study ; from Graeco-Egyptian fragments ; and from the later Byzantine imitations by Eustathius, Theodorus Prodromus,&c., we are left with this catalogue of works commonly comprised under the title of *Erotici Graeci*[1] :

Parthenius.

Iamblichus,   } in Photius's abstract.
Antonius Diogenes,

Achilles Tatius, *Leucippe and Clitophon*.

Longus, *Daphnis and Chloe*.

Xenophon Ephesius, *Habrokomes and Antheia*.

Heliodorus Emesaeus, *Theagenes and Chariclea*.

Charito Aphrodisiensis, *Chaereas and Callirrhoe*.

Of these, Parthenius I have dealt with already: he is no novelist, but a professor 'devilling' for a Romantic poet. With Iamblichus and Antonius Diogenes I am no more concerned except to pick up another remark of Photius. That diligent and learned schismatic ranks Iamblichus midway between Achilles Tatius and Heliodorus in the scale of indecency. (It is only fair to add that the indecency is seldom, if ever, gross; but the whole body of this literature can be assigned to none other than the Fleshly School.) Lucius of Patras is lost (Apuleius's original) ; Damascius, whom he also names, is an *epigonus*, of Justinian's time.

---

[1] The best available texts are Hercher's edition (Teubner) and Boissonade's (Didot).

So after a judicious jettison we are left with five usually admitted specimens of what a Greek novel was. But these are not all: an extremely important addition must be made—Flavius Philostratus's *Apollonius of Tyana*.

The title of the book, not a βίος but τὰ εἰς 'Απολλώνιον, instantly warns us (though the warning has been generally disregarded) that this does not profess to be a biography, and instantly suggests the τὰ κατὰ Λευκίππην καὶ Κλειτοφῶντα, the τὰ περὶ Θεαγένην καὶ Χαρίκλειαν. It is in fact a historical novel written with a purpose. The author by training and by genius inclines to the *Cyropaedia* as a model; and what with his very superior powers, what with the subject prescribed to him by his imperial patroness Julia Domna, produces a novel which stands a good way apart from all the rest. Certainly it is no ἐρωτικόν—anything but; a δραματικόν it is, and fulfils one of Photius's conditions. It owes nothing to poetry, much to Strange Tales of Travel, and all that backstairs literature of credulous fervour and simple-minded curiosity which Reitzenstein so well depicts, and which had at last fought its way to respectability—and to Court, after some such struggle as the vernaculars had to fight with the pride of Latinity in Europe at the last Renascence.

But the *Apollonius* is not the sole example of a survival from the historical didactic romance as attempted in the *Cyropaedia*. Charito's *Chaereas and Callirrhoe* has a background of history—at least of historic names; the lovers' romance is dignified by making Callirrhoe daughter to Hermocrates of Syracuse, and her adventures involve the very King of Persia himself. But there is no more decisive proof of Philostratus's superiority than a comparison of these two books in point of history. His work has been appealed to for a serious authority on the Flavian emperors, while Charito's work presents grave anachronisms in the very scheme ; and the details make no pretence to historicity.

So, whereas it is a long step from Philostratus to Charito, Charito's nominally historical setting removes him very little way from the rest of the novelists ; his history, good or bad, is only a background lightly touched in ; and the main interest is the passionate, the tragically divided, and at last marvellously reconciled loves of a young man and a young woman.

Longus, whose poetical ancestry derives from the Pastoral poets and more particularly from the alliance of Pastoral with Elegy,[1] owes much to the prose pastoral too, of which we have a neglected masterpiece in Dio Chrysostom's *Huntsman*. To the same movement—slightly deflected by contemporary tendencies of Court religion—we owe Philostratus Lemnius's *Heroicus*, Aelian's *Rustic Epistles*, and Alciphron. Longus dates in the Antonine epoch. His work is professedly the interpretation of a picture, but no ordinary ecphrasis.

But all the other novelists are deeply indebted to Flavius Philostratus for the perfection which the expressive arts of language—all that the technical term *Ecphrastic* connotes—realized in his masterly

---

[1] Which we possess, exemplified, scantily but sufficiently in Leonidas Tarentinus.

hands.   He is much the greatest name in this First
Renascence, the Atticist Renascence, which, beginning under the Antonines, matured and closed under
the Severi ; it is thanks to him that Greek regained
an absolute accomplishment and facility of expres-
siveness for subtle and nice phrasing ; and the Novel,
viewed largely, is, in its accomplishment, a phase of
this Atticist Renascence.   The technical terms in
which the Byzantine Scholiasts describe the style of
the novelists, denote just that easy agility, dexterous
sweetness and smoothness, in which Philostratus and
his peers might boast to have renewed—always
bating the otioseness of their matter—the glories of
Plato and Xenophon.   I do not think the influence
of the Philostrati has yet been fully appreciated in
the development of the Novel.[1]

A bit of chronology will not be out of place here
in order to display the new group in its bearings.

Xenophon of Ephesus wrote his *Habrokomes and
Antheia* at some date earlier than A.D. 263.

Heliodorus of Emesa (Racine's favourite) is placed
by W. von Christ at the end of the third century.

Achilles Tatius of Alexandria remains in debate.
By the style I judge him to belong to the later third
century also.   But Suidas says he became a Christian
and a bishop.   A bishop at the Arian Court of
Constantinople might shake hands with those emi-
nent English divines—Laurence Sterne and Jonathan
Swift.   But if Suidas be right, it is difficult to believe
that Achilles could be a pre-Constantinian personage.

---

[1] See introduction to Philostratus's *Apollonius of Tyana* (Oxford
Library of Translations).

Lastly Charito. Charito had been assigned by Rohde, on internal evidence, to the latest place among the novelists, and it was supposed that he was the borrower in all cases of phrase or *motif* common to him and Heliodorus. But Chance does not always play the game. Unluckily for critics, a piece of objective evidence has turned up. Drs. Grenfell and Hunt found a fragment of *Chaereas and Callirrhoe* in a papyrus, which by all the expert tests they pronounced could not be later than the first quarter of the third century, and might be even earlier. All but the highest critics must allow that what is found in a handwriting of the year 200 was composed earlier than the fourth century.

The author of the romance calls himself ' Charito of Aphrodisias (a town in Caria), secretary to Athenagoras the rhetor'. Rohde has found the name Ulpius Charito in a Carian inscription; and nobody now believes that name and place are alike merely symbolic fictions. Since Rohde's date has been upset, some have gaily moved Charito back into Nero's reign: he seems to me to be of the Severian time. One might be tempted to fancy that he is the Charito [1] to whom Fl. Philostratus addresses a letter (xlvi) in these harsh terms: ' You imagine that posterity will remember your writings after you are dead. Writings which do not exist while they are there—what will they be, when they are no more ? '

If so, dismissing Longus, who represents a different

---

[1] His very first sentence is most typically Philostratean in cast. Cf. Vit. Apoll. Tyan. Kays. 336. 15. Also his Greek is not uninfluenced by Latin idiom, like Aelian's.

though an allied genre, it would appear that the typical examples of love romance belong to Philostratus's own period—he lived till after A. D. 244—or to the following two generations during which we know that his influence, and his kinsman's (Lemnius), remained paramount.

It will not do to say so much on the absence, on the gradual coming, on the conditions and causes of the Novel, and give no account of the thing itself. Any one will do equally well for the purpose. If I select Achilles as my specimen, it is because he presents all the typical characteristics in shorter compass than Heliodorus, at least attempts a greater complication of intrigue than Xenophon Ephesius, and is perhaps the best reading of any. This is a very brief account of *Leucippe and Clitophon* :—

The author begins with a description of Sidon. He has reached Sidon after a stormy voyage, and after paying his vows to Astarte is touring round the sights of the city, especially the temples.[1] Among others he remarks a painting of the story of Zeus and Europa, of which he gives us a verbal engraving in the manner of Philostratus's *Imagines*. Nothing was better taught in the literature school than this exercise in pictorial phrasing : five hundred years before the Alexandrian poets had done it admirably in verse, yet hardly better than Homer in the first instance.[2] Where all was good, he found nothing

---

[1] The ex-voto offerings made every great temple a museum of art.

[2] The ecphrasis is notably missing in *Habrokomes and Antheia* ; also the predominance of Fortune is hardly apparent (I. 10). Xenophon is

more excellent in the composition than the figure of
Eros, and ' being a sentimental fellow ' he was scru-
tinizing this and saying ' Think of such a brat being
lord of earth and sea ! ', when a young man who was
standing beside him chimed in with ' I could have
showed *that* : so much outrageous usage have I put
up with from Eros '. The author invites him to
tell his story. The stranger says his story is
strange as a fable ; the author replies that this is
rather a recommendation. And so in a Platonic
scene—a grove of plane-trees, many and leafy, near
a cool translucent stream of water,—they sit down
side by side. Such is the framework. But the
craftsmanship is curiously perfunctory ; for though
the whole story is now told in the first person by the
stranger (who announces himself as Clitophon, a
Greek of Tyre), the author forgets, or at least
neglects, to frame any epilogue answerable to the
introduction ; he ends the book, instead, with the
end of Clitophon's narrative. However, the device
of using narrative in the first person distinguishes
Achilles Tatius from Charito, Xenophon, and Heliodorus, and gives him a certain dramatic advantage. In
Xenophon's *Habrokomes and Antheia* there are more
sub-narratives ; many persons tell each their own story.

Clitophon has been unwillingly betrothed to his
half-sister Calligone, at the age of 19 ; and now
ἤρχετο τοῦ δράματος ἡ τύχη. His uncle Sostratus writes
to say that he is sending his daughter Leucippe and

more directly in debt to the elegists, and has many echoes of Propertian
phrase. Also his enthusiasm for Isis and her worship seems to be
the personal conviction of a devotee, as with Apuleius.

her mother from Byzantium, his home, to Tyre for safety during a war.   This fatal cousin arrives, is seen, and conquers Clitophon.   'Her eye sparkles when she is pleased; she has auburn curly hair [1] and jet black eyebrows' (a rather rare combination, but not unknown in Scotland and Ireland); 'the complexion of her cheek is like ivory touched with crimson dye; her lips like an unfolding rosebud.'

He takes counsel with his cousin Clinias, to whose tragical love affairs (Greek style) we are incidentally treated : his favourite, a charioteer, is killed by a fall from the horse of which Clinias had made him a present.   This gives occasion for that purple patch on a driving accident which seems to have been to Greek and Roman audiences what the fox-hunting joke is to *Punch*.   Assisted by Clinias, Clitophon pursues his courtship, indoors and out, by day and night, by hook and by crook; now the scene is in the garden, which is described with a minuteness that makes a precedent for the copious futility of our lady journalists on this subject.   Indeed, the rhetoric school at its worst is a kind of school of journalism; at its best, it can create something very like d'Annunzio.   Achilles does succeed in producing an atmosphere of Sybaris, just as our modern hellenizing dilettanti do—a Symonds or a d'Annunzio.   His own phrase (p. 70) ἦν δ' ἄνεμος ἡδονῆς characterizes the book.—But we shall never have done if I stop to record each several embellishment, each fable, ecphrasis, dialexis, or miniature meleté which decorates the tenor of the story.   We must stick to the plot.

---

[1] This is usual in heroines: so has Antheia.

Well then, the amorous intrigue runs its course towards an elopement in due form, and the lovers take ship at Berytus, reckless of their destination. The ship is intending for Alexandria. They make friends with an Egyptian fellow passenger called Menelaus, who is travelling to distract his mind from a sorrow very like to that of Clinias. The reader will be prepared for a storm, and after having read thus far he will know that Achilles will write a vivid description : and in fact the storm is very successful. We are duly brought face to face with ' Fear of Death as huge as the expanse of wild sea'. There is a shipwreck. Happily there is no safety in a shipwreck like having a novelist to interest himself in your fortunes. ' The sea was full of dead bodies' —but none of the principals can be spared from the sequel. They are cast on shore at Pelusium, near a temple of Zeus Casius which supplies them with a shelter and the author with another brilliant *Ecphrasis*. We are nearly half-way through the story : the Brigands are due. These brigands are savage *Neatherds* of the Delta, stock figures who appear also in Xenophon and Heliodorus. They are black and brutal. Soldiers rescue Clitophon but not Leucippe, who is carried off. He joins in an attempted rescue against the *Neatherds* and performs prodigies of valour. At the crisis a deep impassable canal divides the attacking force from the main body of brigands, who are 10,000 strong. Across this, powerless to interfere, Clitophon and his allies watch the miscreants preparing and performing a human sacrifice . . . of Leucippe. The horror of it is

suitably displayed in rhetoric.   The body is then
put into a coffin.   Next day the canal is diked and
crossed, and Clitophon hastens to the scene of the
horror, resolved to slay himself on Leucippe's corpse.
He sees two figures in the moonlight . . . Brigands!
Well, they will save him the trouble of suicide.   He
meets them—they prove to be his slave Satyrus and
his late shipmate Menelaus, saved from the wreck.
They assure him Leucippe is alive.   He knocks on
the coffin and is answered by a sound.   They open
it, and she comes out—gashed open and *minus* all
viscera.   These gruesome details are not minimized:
the word γαστήρ is one of Achilles' vices.   Things
look pretty bad: but they cannot be as bad as all that:
and we are soon relieved to learn that Leucippe is
alive: a sheepskin full of entrails, and such a sword
as is used for stabbing on the stage, explain the
mystery.   Clinias is also found to have been saved
from the wreck; and Book III ends with the great
punitive expedition in progress under command of
Charmides.   The next trouble is Charmides falling
in love with Leucippe; he has a philtre administered
to her which drives her mad.   This produces com-
plications.   When these are mended the party goes
to Alexandria, which the author describes with
patriotic enthusiasm.   A birthday feast at Pharos
proves to be a trap and ends in Leucippe being
carried away in a boat by a new rival—Chaereas.
Clitophon pursues in a ship of war: and has the
mortification of seeing Leucippe brought out on the
poop of the pursued vessel and there solemnly
beheaded.   Her head is thrown into the sea, whence

Clitophon recovers it and buries it, making in elegant language all the reflections which a well-educated stylist would have been trained to make on burying a head with a trunk missing. Bad again : but even now we know it is not as bad as it seems. Mere beheading will not hurt a heroine who has triumphantly survived disembowelling by brigands. However, we return to Alexandria.

Six months later, Clitophon, his wound cured, walking in the streets there, meets Clinias : Clinias has been back home to Sidon since the wreck, and has news to impart : the cruel parent had actually betrothed the loving cousins, but the letter was delayed. What irony ! All their troubles and perils for nothing ! Such is the sport of Chance, the divine patroness of the Novel, to whom all these writers make such frequent acknowledgements— and deservedly, for they *do* draw freely on the Unexpected as a resource.

A new interest now begins. Leucippe presumed dead, great siege is laid to Clitophon by Melite, a lovely widow from Ephesus, as amorous as she is lovely, as wealthy as she is amorous. Clitophon accepts her overtures with indifference, but they are betrothed in the temple of Isis and the marriage is to be consummated on their arrival at Ephesus. Delay is irksome to the widow ; on the voyage she is very amorous indeed. They reach Ephesus in six days ; and Clitophon takes a drive in the widow's carriage to view her magnificent estates. Whom should he find there but Leucippe hardly recognizable, with cropped hair and in irons, working in the garden :

she has been sold for a slave. She communicates with Clitophon and is satisfied that he is faithful to her. Meanwhile the widow Melite, disgusted at his coldness, employs Leucippe to prepare a philtre for his improvement.

At this point: enter Enoch Arden—Melite's husband, Thersander, who was not really drowned at sea at all. This makes a great *peripeteia*. Clitophon is beaten and locked up : Thersander is furious with Melite. There is a farewell scene between her and Clitophon, in which at last our hero fails to equal Joseph Andrews. And now the action grows fast and furious : Sosthenes the bailiff praises Leucippe to Thersander: Clitophon, in prison, is told a false tale of her infidelity and Melite's ; he resolves to denounce Melite and die. But Clinias tells all the truth in court. Sosthenes bolts, leaving Leucippe free. A priest of Artemis intervenes : Leucippe's father, Sostratus, intervenes—a most timely embassy brings him to Ephesus. And all ends in the vindication of Leucippe's virginity by a double ordeal—very curious in point of local superstition—of the magic Panpipes and the magic Spring of Rhodôpis. Thersander flees the country ; Sosthenes confesses all ; Leucippe tells her story—it was not her head but somebody else's of the same sex and general appearance that Clitophon had buried. Even Clitophon's half-sister is not forgotten, but married to her cousin Callisthenes.

The last book betrays the rhetoric school in an orgy of speeches : it also contains the only humorous touch in the piece — the worthy old

rector of the temple of Artemis is a great Aristo-
phanic scholar, a discipline which both furnishes
and excuses the wealth of Attic Billingsgate into
which he breaks out when he has been insulted by
Thersander.

To pass a summary judgement on the story: it is
frankly childish—for Oriental things strike us as
childish if they be not frightful. It has no more
attempt at character-drawing or psychology than the
other Romances. But those who read the 1001 Nights
with pleasure must certainly find pleasure in *Clitophon
and Leucippe*.   There is no laughter in it, but a
breathless succession of improbable incident.   Yet
no improbability so great as when, in *Habrokomes
and Antheia*, the crucified hero (bound, not nailed)
is saved by a gale of wind blowing his cross over
into the neighbouring Nile, down which (right
way up!) he securely floats.[1] The literary skill
is not contemptible.   The plot is extravagant
indeed but not incoherent. The prettiness of the
setting in several of the scenes deserves praise.
Pious and enthusiastic Hellenists who have not the
language will say, How Greek! those who know
Greek will say, *How Oriental!* The affectation that
poisons all self-conscious Renascences is in this
Achilles as in the rest. *Talis artifex non pereo* is
their motto. And yet, after all, what a strange
thought—that an Alexandrian with the names of
Achilles Tatius (what a pair!), atticizing *con furore*
in the reign of Diocletian, should write a story which

---

[1] Also in *Chaereas and Callirrhoe* there is a rescue of a crucified
man.

delighted the Byzantine Middle Ages and can still be read with interest and amusement! What a thing is Europe!

We have inspected an example of this latest-born of the genres, which took substance after so many centuries of vicissitude. The Novel is a child of the Greek genius in its senility; it came too late for there to be a great man to exploit its possibilities. I think Rohde was right when he said that there was more pleasure in the inquiry into its origins than in the actual literature when, at long last, we get to it. To borrow Samuel Butler's quaint figure: the 'pestering of the unborn' is what interests us—far back, in Euripides, in Theophrastus, in the Elegists, in Menander. We have watched something that was long an almost ubiquitous yet elusive constituent at last exhibited in the free state, with something of disillusion. And yet the triumphant Novel, a form which after many centuries of modification and transformation is apparently still in full vigour, may condescend to look back at the distant founder of the family, as a modern patrician traces his pedigree proudly to an ancestor who was a scullion in William the Conqueror's kitchen.

POSTSCRIPT

This lecture was written and delivered before Dr. S. L. Wolff's book *The Greek Romances in Elizabethan Prose Fiction* (New York, Columbia University Press, 1912) appeared. The author devotes

235 pages to a very careful and minute account of
the extant Greek novels, before proceeding to table
and analyse their English offspring. This arrangement
makes me the less regret that in the short space of
a single lecture I must needs restrict the descriptive
part in order to make room for a wider cast of critical
adventure in speculations which seemed to me to have
more novelty, more significance, and more promise
of suggestion.   Dr. Wolff's learned volume displays
how much that thesis-writers will not willingly let
die in English Literature was derived from the Greek
novelists, as purveyed to the new curiosity by Italian
scholarship.   But probably their most important
result was in the literature of the *Grand Siècle* in
France.   Brunetière's (posthumous) second volume
of the new History of French Literature indicates a
Greek strain both in the romances (*Le Grand
Cyrus*, &c.) and, what is of more account, the plays of
Racine.

CICERONIANISM

By A. C. Clark

The subject which I propose to treat in this lecture is Cicero's influence upon the life and thought of posterity. The material is vast, and it will be necessary to practise severe compression.

The life of Cicero does not here concern us. The chief facts are known to all. He was the last great statesman of republican Rome, and the two achievements which have made him famous are his suppression of the anarchist Catiline and his gallant attempt to organize the forces of the Commonwealth against Antony. He was a man who fought with words, and when, after his murder, Fulvia took upon her knees the bleeding head and drove a pin from her hair through his tongue, she confessed the unrivalled power of his eloquence.

Cicero himself based his claims to fame upon his speeches. He also wrote a number of treatises upon philosophical and political subjects. Also, he was a great letter-writer. I propose to say a very few words concerning his work in these three departments.

Cicero's speeches must be taken in connexion with his treatises upon the art of rhetoric. They contain the theories which in the speeches he endeavoured to exemplify. The central point in his conception is that oratory is not a mere trick to be learnt by a man of vicious life or imperfect education. The orator must be a good man, he must have a full knowledge of his subject, and must also have mastered all branches of knowledge. When Cicero wrote, there were two styles contending for the mastery, the Asiatic and the Attic. The first was florid, with a tendency to bombast, and so rhythmical as to resemble a chant. The second avoided all decoration, with the result that it became bald and bloodless. Cicero aimed at the happy mean between these extremes.

Cicero's treatises on philosophy and politics did not profess to be original. They were written during intervals in a busy life and chiefly during periods of dejection, when he wanted some occupation to relieve his mind. He tells us himself that he copied Greek authors with freedom, and there is no doubt that they contain much that is mere translation. They were not rated highly by himself or by the Romans of the empire. They possess, however, extreme importance to the historian, since they have had greater influence upon life and thought than any other works upon philosophy, whether ancient or modern. This is due to two reasons: the magic of his style, and the point of view from which they are written.

Cicero did not belong to either of the great schools of the period, namely, the Stoics and Epicureans, but followed the methods of the New Academy, which avoided all dogma and system, listened to all arguments for and against, and was content to accept for the time the conclusion which seemed most probable. I can only indicate briefly some points which have been most fruitful in his writings. Cicero based his conviction of divine existence upon the consent of mankind and ideas innate in the soul of man. He defended the freedom of the will against fatalism, and disbelieved in omens and divination. In morals he held that each man is the architect of his own virtue. He was a strong individualist, and maintained the right of each man to develop upon his own lines and do that for which he is best fitted. He was the champion of free-thought, free-will, and individualism.

Cicero wrote a vast quantity of letters, many of which have perished. Of those which remain, 916 in number, if we include a number of letters written to himself, the most interesting are those written to Atticus, his closest friend. These were not meant for publication, they were never revised, and do not appear to have been published until about ninety years after his death. In these Cicero confesses all his feelings of the moment and lays bare his very soul. Thanks to them, we know Cicero as we know no other person in the ancient world.

With the exception of these letters all the writings of Cicero exhibit one peculiar style. A characteristic of this which has been noticed by all critics is 'fullness'. Quintilian says that it is impossible to take anything from Demosthenes or to add anything to Cicero (X. i. 106). Longinus says, 'Demosthenes' strength is in sheer height of sublimity, that of Cicero is in its diffusion. Demosthenes because he burns and ravages all in his violence, swift, strong, terrible, may be compared to a lightning flash or a thunderbolt. Cicero like a spreading conflagration ranges and rolls over the whole field : the fire which burns is within him, plentiful and constant, distributed at his will, now in this part, now in another, and fed by fuel in relays.'[1]

Cicero's fullness largely depends on his use of the period. This is the feature of his style which is most easily caricatured, and its use by unskilful imitators has led to much prejudice. The period was, of course, no new invention, but had been developed by a succession of Greek writers. The justification of the period is that it is an attempt to express in language the complexity of thought. This is achieved by a number of subordinate clauses which are combined in the unity of the sentence. Conflicting factors are set forth which are naturally expressed in balanced antitheses and clauses of equal length. Periodic prose has many points of resemblance to lyric poetry, falling into strophes and antistrophes. Further, a carefully constructed sentence must be not only logical, but also musical. This brings us to the inmost secret of Cicero's prose, that its music is more perfect than that of any other writer at any period. The ancients were greatly interested in the theory of prose-rhythm, and Cicero in particular has discussed it at length, giving illustrations from his own works, where the slightest variation in the order destroyed the rhythm. To put the matter as simply as possible. The Greeks and Romans thought certain cadences more musical than others, and were accustomed to use them at the most sensitive points of the sentence, namely, at the end and wherever previously the speaker stopped to draw breath. They gave the

[1] Ch. 12. 4, tr. Prickard.

name of colon to a clause and of comma to a smaller subdivision. We punctuate by stops, they did so by cadences.

A further point to notice is that Cicero did not always use long sentences. He recommends that these should be varied by short sentences. 'We must not confine ourselves to the broadsword, but should sometimes employ the dagger.'[1]

The imitators of Cicero in English have chiefly erred from failure to recognize these points, the most noticeable case being that of Johnson, who never used the 'dagger', and whose ears seem deaf to music. Cicero's rhythm is better reproduced by Sir Philip Sidney, who was keenly sensitive to this as a feature in Cicero's style, or at a later date by Gibbon, who, after leaving Oxford, read the whole of Cicero, and exhibits a well-marked rhythm in his rolling sentences.

Latin prose did not develop on the lines laid down by Cicero. The Attic and Asiatic schools continued to strive for the mastery. In the time of Augustus the circle of Pollio, who belonged to the first of these schools, was bitterly hostile to Cicero. Later on the Asiatic school became predominant, and Seneca, who 'taught philosophy the language of passion', was regarded as the only philosopher. Writers of the Silver Age wrote in epigrams, and criticized Cicero because he did not furnish the reader with quotations or extracts. There are signs of a revulsion under Vespasian, and Quintilian in particular was a devoted admirer of Cicero, whom he considers the chief figure

---

[1] *Orator*, § 224.

in Latin literature. He was, however, merely regarded as a stylist and his writings had no influence
upon human life. The spirit of Cicero, strange as
it may seem, was first revivified by the diffusion of
Christianity.

We find in the second century A.D. two views of
heathen literature. The first is that of Tertullian.
'What is there in common between Athens and
Jerusalem, between the Academy and the Church ?
We need no curiosity after the coming of Jesus Christ,
no inquiry after the teaching of the Gospel. When
we believe, we do not desire to believe anything beyond.' So also, he says, 'beware of those who have
devised a Stoic, a Platonic or dialectical Christianity.'
If this view had prevailed, the teaching of Cicero
must have been blotted out, since it was only in such
a form of Christianity that it could find any place.
The other view is voiced by the learned Platonist,
Clement of Alexandria, who compares the obscuran-
tists to the sailors of Odysseus who stop their ears
with wax so that they may not hear the song of the
Sirens, 'Come unto us, much-wandering Odysseus . . .
we know all that shall happen on the fruitful earth.'
The comparison was very just. The wisdom of the
ancients was a Siren song. The Church did not stop
her ears and was possessed by the haunting melody.
The first apologetic work of the Christian Church
was the so-called 'pearl of Christian Latin', the
Octavius of Minucius Felix. In this dialogue, which
is Ciceronian in form, argument, and thought, the
speakers are Caecilius the heathen and Octavius the
Christian. Caecilius argues that reason can tell us

nothing of the gods, and that it is best to acquiesce in the national religion. Octavius borrows from Cicero arguments used by the Stoics, for example, that from 'design', to prove the existence of a creator, and shows that philosophy and revelation agree. 'We must hold', says he, 'either that the Christians are now philosophers, or that the philosophers of old were Christians.' He makes a bolder use of the sceptical weapons found in the armoury of Cicero, reproducing his arguments against divination, and declaring that prodigies are impossible. ' If they took place in the past, they would take place still. Since they are impossible, they never took place.' So also the tales of the sons and daughters of the gods must be untrue, since they have no sons or daughters now. These arguments against the miraculous are singular in the mouth of a Christian, and many must have felt that Christianity had found a dangerous ally.

The Christian writers at the end of the third century, and throughout the fourth, followed on the whole in the path of Minucius, not in that of Tertullian. Thus, Arnobius, referring to the destruction of Christian books by the Pagans, says that, to be logical, they should also burn those of Cicero, which are full of similar arguments. His disciple, Lactantius, ' the Christian Cicero,' was saturated with reminiscences of his prototype. He says that Cicero was a perfect philosopher as well as orator, and finds in him anticipations of Christian teaching. Thus he refers to the ' wellnigh inspired utterance' of Cicero in *De re publica* iii. 3, when he founds morality upon

the 'law of God written in every human heart'. He
also makes use of the negative side of Cicero's teaching, and boldly declares that the arguments used in
the third book of the *De natura deorum* destroy all
religiones, a statement afterwards repeated, though
with a different application, by Voltaire.

At the end of the fourth century the Church is no
longer suffering, but triumphant. It was only natural
that Christian writers should feel some scruples concerning the teaching of the great free-thinker who
had been their ally in their onslaughts upon Paganism.
The chief names are those of St. Jerome (340-420),
St. Ambrose (340-397), and St. Augustin (354-430).
St. Jerome tells us that, after he had surrendered all
earthly ties, he could not bring himself to part with
the library which he had collected with such zeal, and
that he sinned by reading Cicero even on fast-days.
He was once seized by a fever and given up for dead.
While lying unconscious, he was in a vision brought
before the judgement-seat and asked, 'What art
thou?' He goes on, 'I replied, "A Christian." The
voice came back, " No, thou art not a Christian, but
a Ciceronian, since where thy treasure is, there is thy
heart also."' Then he fell on his face, and swore
that never again would he keep, or read, books containing worldly wisdom. After this promise he rallied
and was cured of his malady.[1] St. Jerome rated his
strength too highly. The Siren's song never ceased
to haunt him, and he was taunted with perjury by
a rival, who said, 'Whence comes your fluency, your
brilliancy of thought, your power of expression? If

[1] *Epist.* xxii. 30.

I am not mistaken, you still read Cicero in secret.'
Jerome replies that his promise was only for the
future. He cannot blot out of his mind what he has
learnt: to do this he must needs drink the waters of
Lethe of which the poets tell.

St. Ambrose was a devoted student of Cicero. He
wrote a work, *De Officiis ministrorum*, founded and
modelled on Cicero's *De Officiis*, which remained for
centuries the chief Christian manual upon morals.
This treatise was not an imitation of Cicero, but
a translation of Cicero into the language of Christianity. It was through the work of St. Ambrose that
Cicero's moral philosophy passed into the Christian
Church. The horizon of St. Ambrose is more narrow
than that of Minucius and Lactantius, and we feel
ourselves perceptibly nearer the Middle Ages. Thus,
he asks, ' How can any rule of morals be allowed for
which there is not support in the New or Old Testa-
ments? For every point it is necessary to find
a text or an example in Scripture.' But in practice
he is more indulgent than in theory, and many
difficulties are solved by liberal use of allegory.
' Cicero', he says, ' has taught that faith is the foundation of justice (*Off*. i. 23). Can any one doubt that
Isaiah thought the same? He says, in Sion I lay
a foundation : this is, Christ the foundation of the
Church. Christ, therefore, is the faith, and the Church
is a form of justice.'

While St. Ambrose Christianized Cicero, Cicero
converted an unbeliever to Christianity. The convert
was no less a person than St. Augustin, who thus tells
his story : ' When a frivolous youth, I studied books

on eloquence, in which I desired to gain distinction, and I chanced in the ordinary course of school reading to open a book of Cicero, whose style all admire, though not his spirit. The work in question urges us to study philosophy, and is called *Hortensius*. This book changed my feelings and turned me to pray before thee, and altered all my prayers and desires. Suddenly all my empty hopes lost their charm. I longed for eternal wisdom with a strange yearning at my heart and I essayed to rise, to return to thee.'[1] Not without reason does Augustin, when commenting upon the Epistle of St. Peter, express the hope that among the 'spirits in prison', to whom Christ preached at the descent into hell, may have been some of those 'whom I know and love on account of their writings, who were honoured by men on account of their eloquence and their wisdom'.

The relations of St. Augustin to Cicero are of special interest, since various cardinal points in the philosophy of Cicero are in direct conflict with the teaching of Augustin. Not only was this so, but on each point Cicero agreed with the heretic Pelagius, not with the Catholic Church. Cicero taught that virtue was the result of human effort, not of divine grace, and this saying sums up the Pelagian view. Cicero held that human nature was good. Augustin replies to the Pelagians, who took the same view, that, if so, Christ died in vain. Cicero upheld the freedom of the will. Augustin refers to this 'detestable view' which exempts man from the divine pre-

[1] *Confess.* iii. 4.

science, and says that since the Fall man has only free will when he offends, otherwise grace is required. Above all, Cicero's assertion of the right to choose (αἵρεσις) on the part of individuals must necessarily be repugnant to the Church which branded such attempts with the terrible name of heresy.

St. Ambrose had attempted to Christianize Cicero : Pelagius set Cicero above Christ. The attitude of Augustin represents a compromise. While in matters of dogma he joins condemnation of Cicero with that of Pelagius, in matters of morals he has to adopt much from Cicero. Also, after this period, the influence of Cicero is felt in a more subtle form. The Pelagians were the last who drew directly from Cicero's writings. Succeeding ages used Lactantius, the Offices of St. Ambrose, and the works of St. Augustin himself, and imbibed ideas of Cicero without their knowledge. As a philosopher he was little read except in certain favourite works, such as the *Offices* and the *Tusculan Disputations*. To the Middle Ages he was in the first place a writer on rhetoric. The taste of the period was very bad. The two treatises which enjoyed the widest circulation were the *De inventione*, written by Cicero at the age of eighteen, and the *Topics*, a translation from Aristotle made by him from memory while on board ship, while a work not by Cicero, but formerly attributed to him, *Ad Herennium*, was still more generally read. On the other hand, the *De Oratore*, Cicero's great work, suffered comparative neglect, while the *Brutus*, in which he traces the development of oratory at Rome, has only come down to us by an accident. The speeches were not much read, with the exception of the *Catilinariae* and the *Caesarianae*, with which may be coupled two spurious invectives supposed to have been exchanged between Cicero and Sallust. Thus several well-known orations have come to us through a single MS., for example, *Pro Sex. Roscio* and *Pro Murena*. France was the country in which the study of the speeches chiefly survived. There in the tenth century Gerbert, afterwards Pope Silvester II, urges a friend to take about with him when travelling 'the numerous speeches written on behalf of many men by the father of Roman elo-quence'. Cicero, as a letter-writer, had little interest for the Middle Ages. The letters *ad Familiares* were occasionally transcribed, but those to Atticus are only mentioned once in mediaeval catalogues, in that of Cluni in Burgundy. During this time some of his most famous works perished, for example, the *Hortensius*, which was not saved by its connexion with St. Au-gustin; the *De Gloria*, for which the Renaissance scholars sought with peculiar ardour; and the *De re publica*, of which only a fragment,—'The Dream of Scipio,'—preserved by Macrobius, was known, until in the last century Cardinal Mai discovered other portions in a palimpsest.

The chief figure in Latin literature throughout the Middle Ages was Virgil, who was considered to have foretold the coming of the Messiah in his fourth Eclogue, and to have expounded under the person of Aeneas the wanderings of the human soul. The tendency of mediaevalism was to assert authority, to inculcate humility and self-repression, and to teach

the valuelessness of worldly wisdom.   There was no
room for individualism or freedom of thought. Dante
is in this respect thoroughly mediaeval. Livy is
praised for his infallibility—*che non erra*—and the
love of glory, Cicero's favourite motive, is one of
the sins punished in the *Inferno*. He shows no
knowledge of Cicero's works beyond those which
were generally read in the Middle Ages.

The early Renaissance was the work of one man,
Petrarch. Time does not allow me to dwell upon the
character of this singular genius, or to explain the
fascination which he exercised upon his contemporaries. Let it suffice to say that he broke with
mediaevalism in two ways. The first was his attitude towards the ancient authors. In the Middle
Ages Latin literature was dead. The central fact
was that the writers were pagans, and therefore under
condemnation. No one sought in them wisdom or
a rule of life. To Petrarch they became living men,
and the sages in whom all knowledge was to be
found. Once more the chant of the Sirens fills the
air, 'We know all that shall be on the fruitful
earth.' Petrarch moves in an imaginary world, com-
muning with the ancients, and above all with Cicero,
' my Cicero,' as he fondly calls him. The second
point is that he discarded the mediaeval ideals of
humility and submission. He is an individualist who
asserts the right of each man to develop his own
powers, and his predominant motive is the love of
glory. For such a man Cicero was naturally the
chief source of inspiration.

It would be a mistaken view to suppose that

Petrarch's love for Cicero was but an incident in his worship of the classics. The truth would seem to be that his devotion to Cicero came first, and that his interest in other authors was secondary. We may therefore say that the Renaissance itself was the work of Cicero's spirit.

Petrarch tells us that his interest in Cicero dated from early boyhood. He says, ' Although at that age I could not understand the meaning, I was charmed by the sweetness and music of the language, which made anything else which I read or heard seem harsh and discordant.' When he was studying law at Montpellier, he used to spend much time in reading Cicero, as well as Virgil and other Latin poets. On one occasion he was surprised by his father, who took his books and threw them into the fire. ' I had been afraid of this,' he says, ' and had previously concealed my treasures ; now they were discovered and before my eyes thrown into the fire as if they had been heretical works. I wept as if I had shared their fate. My father then, seeing my tears, took out of the fire two books already blackened by the flame, and, holding out to me in one hand the Rhetoric of Cicero and in the other Virgil, said, Take Virgil to amuse yourself from time to time and Cicero to help you study civil law.' [1]

Throughout his life Petrarch sought for works of Cicero with great zeal. When twenty-five years of age he discovered at Liège the speech *Pro Archia*, and read with delight the splendid panegyric of

[1] *Rerum Senilium* xv. 1.

literature which it contains. But his greatest
triumph was in 1345, when he discovered at Verona
the letters to Atticus. This discovery was a decisive moment in the history of the Renaissance,
and from it all modern study of Cicero dates. In
the Middle Ages Cicero had been a dim figure, a
shadowy name, the 'god of eloquence'; hence-
forward he was a personality, very human, fallible
and lovable.

It was at first somewhat of a shock to Petrarch
when he found that his hero was a mere man, and
he has recorded his feelings in an imaginary letter
to Cicero:

'I read greedily thy letters, for which I had long
made search, and which I found where I least expected to do so. I heard thee uttering many words,
making many complaints, frequently changing thy
tone. Previously I knew what lessons thou hadst
given to others; now I knew what thou wast like
thyself. Listen now in turn to this lament, I will
not call it advice, wheresoever thou art, which one
of thy descendants, devoted to thy name, pours
forth with many tears. Thou restless and anxious,
or to speak to thee in thy own words, thou headlong
and ill-starred elder, why wouldest thou take part in
so many feuds that could profit thee nought? Why
didst thou renounce the leisure which befitted thy
years, thy profession, and thy state of life? Why
did the false glamour of glory entangle thee at
thine age in the battles of young warriors, and
hurry thee after many hazards to a death unworthy
of a philosopher? Alas, forgetful of thy brother's
warning and of all the wholesome rules which thou
didst thyself lay down, like a wayfarer at night
bearing a lantern in the darkness, thou didst show

a path for them that came after thee to take, and thyself fell in piteous fashion. . . . I grieve as a friend for thy sake, I feel shame and pity for thy frailties, and now, like Brutus, I think nothing of the acquirements in which, as I know, thou didst excel. What profits it to teach others, to speak continually of virtue in chosen language, if all the while thou dost not listen to thine own words? Better had it been for thee, the philosopher, to have grown old in the quiet country, thinking, as thou somewhere dost say, of eternity, not of this short life, never to have held the rods of office, never to have coveted triumphs, not to have been puffed up by the thought of Catiline. But this is all too late now. Farewell, for ever, dear Cicero. Written in the upper world on the right bank of the Adige, in the town of Verona, June xvi, in the year 1345 from the birth of that God whom thou knewest not.'

Six months later Petrarch felt that he had been too harsh, and in a second letter he says :

'My reproaches concerned only thy life, not thy genius or thy eloquence. I marvel at thy genius, and would fain have thy eloquence. Further, the only fault which I have to find with thy life is that I do not find in it the resolution which befits a sage.'[1]

The quest for Cicero's works begun by Petrarch was continued by his successors, and within some fifty years after his death the process of discovery was complete. The chief part was played by Poggio, who at the time of the Council of Constance discovered a number of new speeches in the monasteries of France and Switzerland.

[1] *Ad viros illustres Epist.* i, ii.

We now come to a new period, that of Ciceronianism in the strict sense, namely, the imitation of
Cicero's style. This had not been attempted by
the first generation of Renaissance scholars, and
was contrary to the principle of individualism which
was a cardinal point with Petrarch, as with Cicero.
Petrarch himself lays stress on the fact that his
Latin is that of Petrarch, not of Cicero. The letters
of Poggio, again, are thoroughly characteristic and
possess a style of their own. Latin was still a living
tongue, more literary than scholastic Latin, but
essentially modern and capable of fresh development
to express new ideas. With the spread of education schoolmasters came to the front who, being
themselves lacking in originality, proceeded to copy
the style of the ancients, and, above all, of Cicero.
Their leading principles were (1) Latin can only be
learnt by imitation, (2) it is not possible to imitate
more than one person, (3) that person should be the
best model, (4) the best model is Cicero. Some of
the greatest scholars raised their voices on the other
side. Thus Valla, the boldest spirit of the fifteenth
century, ventured to set up Quintilian against
Cicero, a blasphemous view at which a shriek of
horror arose throughout Italy. On the whole, however, Ciceronianism triumphed, and the triumph
was most complete in ecclesiastical circles. The
protagonist in this movement was Cardinal Bembo,
of whom the words heard by St. Jerome in his
vision may be used, *Ciceronianus non Christianus.*
As previously St. Ambrose had translated Cicero
into the language of Christianity, the clergy of the

fifteenth century restate Christian doctrine in the language of Cicero.

The revolt came from the North and was voiced by Erasmus, who in 1528 published his *Ciceronianus*, in which he attacks not Cicero but the Ciceronians. He says : (1) ' Cicero cannot be imitated because his style is so personal, and because it exactly expresses the ideas of the time in which he lived. Can it be Ciceronian to use language which no longer expresses our ideas ? (2) Cicero ought not to be imitated, since imitation leads to caricature. We ought to preserve the spirit of Cicero, but not sacrifice our individuality. We have not all the works of Cicero, and so cannot be sure if a use is Ciceronian or not. Cicero did not know everything in his own day, and since then the times have changed.' The elder Scaliger replied by a treatise in which he calls Erasmus ' illiterate, a drunkard, an impostor, an apostate, a hangman, a demon hot from hell '.

The impeachment that the Humanists converted Latin into a dead language must hold good. On the other hand, the study of ancient literature had a quickening influence upon Italian prose. This before the Renaissance had been rude and devoid of literary merit. It was from the classical authors, and especially from Cicero, that the Italians learnt the nature and the possibilities of artistic writing in prose. Boccaccio was the founder of Italian prose, and it is significant that, next to Petrarch, he was the greatest scholar of the age.

The true Ciceronians of the Renaissance were those who derived inspiration from him, not those who copied his language; who looked on him as a leader, not as a lord. From this point of view, Valla, who exposed the legend of Constantine's donation, and applied textual criticism to the New Testament itself, was more deeply permeated with the spirit of Cicero than Cardinal Bembo. The spirit of scepticism was now in the air and the world was ready for the Reformation.

In this great movement, as in the counter-Reformation which succeeded it, Ciceronianism plays little part. The individualism of Cicero was repugnant to Catholicism, while Protestantism could not be friendly to one who seemed half-heathen and half-Catholic. Calvin in particular, whose system was based upon predestination, was hostile to one who asserted the freedom of the will and looked on man as the maker of his own virtue. Luther, it is true, took a more kindly view, as is shown by a passage in his Table-talk where he sets Cicero above Aristotle.

'Cicero is greatly superior to Aristotle in philosophy and in teaching. The Offices of Cicero are greatly superior to the Ethics of Aristotle, and although Cicero was involved in the cares of government and had so much on his shoulders, yet he greatly excels Aristotle, who was a lazy ass and cared for nothing but money and possessions and comfortable easy days. Cicero handled the greatest and best questions in his philosophy, such as, Is there a God? What is God? Does He give heed to the actions of men? Is the soul immortal? Aristotle is a good and skilful dialectician, who has observed the right and orderly method in teaching, but the kernel of matters he has not touched. Let those who wish to see a true philosophy read Cicero. Cicero was a wise and industrious man, and he suffered much and accomplished much. I hope that our Lord God will be gracious to him and to the like of him.'[1]

I now come to the third great period of upheaval, which began with the development of free-thought in England and culminated in the French Revolution. In this also we shall find the influence of Cicero to be paramount.

The study of Cicero was zealously prosecuted in England at the time of Queen Elizabeth. Roger Ascham, private tutor to the Queen as a girl, says that when sixteen years of age she had read with him nearly the whole of Cicero, and notes her mastery of periodic and rhythmical prose. In his *Schoolmaster* (1571) he bases his system of education on translation and retranslation from Cicero's letters, according to the method recommended by Cicero in the case of Greek. He says:

'Therefore thou that shootest at perfection in the Latin tonge, thinke not thyself wiser than Tullie was in choice of the way that leadeth rightly to the same, thinke not thy witte better than Tullie's was, as though that may serve thee that was not sufficient for him. For even as a hauke flieth not hie with one wing, even so a man reacheth not to excellency with one tonge.'[2]

On another occasion, after saying 'now I purpose

---

[1] *Table Talk*, 2873.
[2] *Ascham's Works*, ed. Bennett, p. 308.

a little by the way to play and sporte with my master Tullie', he remarks :

' But now, master Cicero, blessed be God and his sonne Jesus Christ, whom you never knew, except it were as it pleased him to lighten you by some shadow . . . that sixteen hundred years after you were dead and gone, it may trewly be said that . . . for learning, beside the knowledge of all learned tonges and liberal sciences, even your own bookes, Cicero, be as well read, and your excellent eloquence is as well liked and loved, and as trewly folowed in Englande at this day, as it is now, or ever was since your own tyme, either at Arpinum, where you was borne, or els at Rome, where you was brought up. And a little to brag with you, Cicero, where you yourselfe, by your leave, halted in some point of learnyng in your own tonge, many in Englande at this day go streight up, both in trewe skill and right doing therein.' [1]

Among those English scholars of whom Roger Ascham speaks the most famous was Sir Philip Sidney, whose favourite author was Cicero. Although, however, his own style was deeply influenced by Cicero, whose music he has caught better than other English imitators, he, like Erasmus, protests against those who ' keep Nizolian paper-books of figures and phrases' instead of imbibing his spirit and ' devouring him whole'. Of Ciceronian tags he says :

' For now they cast sugar and spice upon every dish that is served up to the table : like those Indians not content to wear earrings at the fit and natural place of the ears, but they will thrust jewels through

[1] *Ib.* p. 332.

their nose and lips, because they will be sure to be fine.'

He calls Ciceronianism in the narrow sense the great abuse of Oxford, where *dum verba sectantur, res ipsas negligunt.*[1] So Bacon says:

'This grew speedily to an excess, for men began to hunt more after words than matter: more after the ... round and clean composition of the sentence and the sweet falling of the clauses and the varying and illustrating of their works with tropes and figures than after the weight of matter. . . . Here, therefore, is the first distemper of learning when men study words, not matter.'

The influence of Cicero is most evident in the long line of English philosophers during the seventeenth and eighteenth centuries, who are generally known as Deists, Rationalists, or Freethinkers. The first of these was Lord Herbert of Cherbury, 'the Father of Deism,' who wrote under James I, and the most notable among his successors were Tindall, Toland, Shaftesbury, Bolingbroke, Collins, Locke, and Hume. Deism was an attitude of mind, not a body of doctrine, and the Deists differed both in their views and in their line of argument. Their teaching was partly positive and partly negative, and in course of time the negative side became more prominent.

The positive side of their teaching was that there is a natural religion founded upon notions which are innate in the human mind and witnessed to by the evidence of design in nature. The negative element appears in the tendency to eliminate the supernatural

---

[1] *Defense of Poesy*, ed. A. S. Cook, pp. xvii, 53.

from Christianity with the object of identifying it with
this natural religion.

Lord Herbert founds his system on the Ciceronian
arguments of common notions, innate thoughts, and
universal consent.   He rejects the doctrine that man,
since the Fall, is a ' mass of perdition ', and insists
upon the freedom of the will.   Thus he passes by
Calvin and St. Augustin and stretches out his hand
to his predecessors, Pelagius and Cicero.   Time
does not allow me to linger over the works of his
successors, and it must suffice to say that Cicero is
the author whom they quote most freely.   Among
the most notable of their works may be mentioned
Toland's *Christianity not mysterious* (1695) and
Tindall's *Christianity as old as the Creation* (1730).
Toland says that there are no facts or doctrines
in Christianity or revelation which are not plain
and reasonable ; that there is nothing in them
contrary to reason or incomprehensible.   Tindall
declares that true religion must be founded on
nature and reason, so Christianity must be perfectly reasonable, and its mission is to deliver men
from superstition.   Both writers called themselves
' Christian deists ', and in the same spirit another well-
known deist, Collins, says that ' ignorance is the
foundation of atheism and freethinking the cure of it '.
Hume, who comes at the end of the movement,
declares that he had Cicero's *De Officiis* before him
in all his thoughts, and his dialogue on Natural
Religion is modelled on Cicero's tract *De natura
deorum*.   In it the argument from design is found
insufficient, but the writer falls back on the Ciceronian

position, that the conviction of divine existence is one
which cannot be torn out from the soul of man.

Voltaire stood in close connexion with English
rationalism. He had, indeed, spent three years in
England and was a friend of Bolingbroke. He had
an unbounded admiration for Cicero, whom he found
a useful ally in his contest with the Church. Thus,
in setting forth views of his own, he put them in the
form of letters from Memmius to Cicero, supposed
to have been found in the Vatican library by a Russian
prince, who had translated them into Russian, from
which language they had been translated into French
by himself. On another occasion he tells a story of
an embassy sent by Rome to the Emperor of China.
The monarch put questions to the envoys concerning
the religion of their country, and was most unfavour-
ably impressed by their account. When, however,
he heard that a certain Cicero, their greatest orator
and philosopher, had written a book in which he
covered with ridicule the whole system of auspices
and divination, he had this translated into Chinese,
and after reading it became the faithful friend of
Rome.[1]

The influence of Cicero as a model for orators was
felt in England earlier than elsewhere. This was
doubtless due to the existence in England of two insti-
tutions not found on the Continent, namely, trial by
jury and free debate in the House of Commons. It
would be a long task to trace the history of Ciceronianism in the law courts and in Parliament, and the
materials have not yet been collected. Campbell, in

[1] *Remarques de l'esprit sur les mœurs*, iv.

his *Lives of the Chancellors*, tells us that Shaftesbury was the first great parliamentary debater, and, as such, was unequalled until the days of Chatham. His dexterous appeals to party feeling and epigrammatic turns are contrasted with the monotonous divisions and subdivisions of Pym, and the cant and pedantry of speakers in the Long Parliament. We must remember in this connexion that Shaftesbury was a devoted student of Cicero. The golden age of Ciceronianism in Parliament came a century later, when the great orators turned to Rome and Athens for inspiration. It is impossible to read the speeches of Chatham, Pitt, Sheridan, Fox, and Burke without recognizing their debt to Cicero and Demosthenes. The most striking example is to be found in Burke's impeachment of Warren Hastings, which is modelled upon Cicero's indictment of Verres. It is interesting in this connexion to notice Dr. Johnson's somewhat fretful criticism, as recorded by Boswell.

'Dr. Johnson, when asked what the particular excellence of Burke's eloquence was, said, "Copiousness and fertility of allusion, a power of diversifying his matter by putting it in various relations."

Boswell. Do you think, Sir, that Burke has read Cicero much?

Johnson. I don't believe it, Sir. Burke has great knowledge, great fluency, and great promptness of ideas, so that he can speak with great illustration on any subject which comes before him. He is neither like Cicero nor Demosthenes, nor like any one else, but speaks as well as he can.'

Dr. Johnson did not notice that the 'copiousness'

which he attributed to Burke was the chief characteristic of Cicero's style, as was pointed out by
Quintilian. Possibly he regarded the imitation of
Cicero as his own monopoly, and felt some pro-
fessional jealousy towards a rival. It is obvious to
any classical scholar that Burke has caught the spirit
of Cicero with peculiar success.

The French republicans, treading in the steps of
Voltaire, worshipped Cicero with peculiar ardour.
To them he was in the first place a political thinker
and an orator, from whose writings they drew in their
struggle against monarchy, and whom they set before
themselves as a model of style. Thus Mably, whose
work on the rights and duties of a citizen received
the approbation of the Constituent Assembly, says
of him, ' I prefer to err with Cicero than to find the
truth with other philosophers.' In the treatise to
which I refer, which is said to mark the first stage in
the Revolution, he quotes a passage from Cicero's
Laws in support of his thesis that ' a citizen is not
bound to obey tyrants '.[1] In France trial by jury
dates from 1790. The advocates and politicians had
no models of forensic eloquence in their own literature and turned to Cicero, whom they copied with
singular *naïveté*. Thus Mirabeau, in a speech of this
period, founds his oration on the second Catilinarian,
in which Cicero classifies the enemies of the country
and shows their inferiority to the forces of order. He
combines with this imitations of a passage in the *Pro
Milone* (§ 1), in which Cicero complains of the presence
of troops at the trial, and one from the *Pro Ligario*

[1] *Leg.* 1. 42.

(§15), in which Cicero contrasts the clemency of Caesar with the cruelty of his advisers. The republicans always had Rome before their eyes. 'Since the times of the Romans the world is empty,' said St. Just. 'This was the way of the Romans' was a frequent saying in the Republican clubs, and the guillotine itself was commended as being a Roman invention. The orators all talk of Cicero and Catiline: the difficulty was to know which was which. The Girondins called Robespierre Catiline, and a member of the party delivered what Madame Roland calls a 'Catilinarian' against him, in which he was accused, like Catiline, of conspiracy against the State and of plotting to burn the capital. Robespierre thus assailed from Cicero went to Cicero for defence, and after a week's interval replied by a speech modelled on Cicero's *Pro Sulla*, in which Cicero defends a client accused of complicity with Catiline. On the other hand Robespierre posed as Cicero himself, the vigorous governor who suppressed the enemies of the State, and was dubbed Cicero in the *chansons* of the day.

It will be seen from this brief sketch that the world has regarded Cicero differently during the great periods of transition which we have considered. The early Church saw in him only the philosopher, and was chiefly interested in the positive side of his teaching. The Renaissance was attracted by his personality as revealed in his letters, and inspired by his assertion of man's right to develop his individuality. The Rationalists directed their attention to the negative side of his philosophy, and endeavoured to identify

Christianity with natural religion. The Revolution saw in him the orator and statesman, the champion of freedom against despotism. The spirit of Cicero is not dead, but still moves among us and delivers a message to those that hearken. What, however, that message is at the present day, and what we have still to learn from Cicero, is a large subject which I cannot now discuss.

NOTE.—This lecture, which was not originally intended for publication, is based on Zielinski's *Cicero im Wandel der Jahrhunderte*, ed. ii, Leipzig, 1908.

VERGIL

By H. W. Garrod

Let me begin by apologizing for a title which seems
to promise everything, but which brings with it,
I fear, nothing of any comprehension or completeness.
I hesitated among several titles, and I chose finally
that one which left me most free.   In so wide a subject I must have liberty to wander.   I cannot hope to
explore fully any single path of it, still less to make
any ordered survey of the whole. The best that I can
hope to do is here and there to lift the fringes of the
forest, to open out glimpses of avenues that are
infinite, to give some suggestion of depths and glooms
which it would be rash and profane to attempt to
penetrate more intimately.

It is unlikely that of a poet who has had the
admiration and study of twenty centuries I shall have
anything to say that will be very new—or that, if
I had, it would be true.   It is unlikely ; nor will you
want it : since, if I understand rightly what is expected
of me, I am not asked to speak to you as a scholar
speaking to scholars, but rather as a student of ancient
poetry speaking to students of modern poetry.   I am
asked to speak to you, not as an expositor of anti-
quarian learning, but as one who, mindful of the
continuity of Literature, but a lingerer by habit at its
sources, finds himself among those whose steps follow

more familiarly the broader reaches. You wish to
hear not the new things—if there be any—about
Vergil, but the old ones ; not the little things (which
are most the scholar's concern, and which are all he has
that is new) but the great ones. What does Vergil
mean in the history of literature, in the unresting
movement of the human imagination ; what is the
secret of an influence which has extended beyond
poetry into all literature, into religion and into life,
into the life not merely of individuals but of nations ?

It is this that you wish to hear about. I use the
word 'secret'. Yet it is perhaps inappropriate.
What I have to offer towards the interpretation of
this 'secret' will, at any rate, have no esoteric character—the κλῃδοῦχοι are mostly quacks, and in the
temple of Poetry there is no one person appointed to
lock and unlock, to conceal and reveal. The secret
of a great poet is in the keeping of many generations
of men ; and I shall not attempt, in what follows, to
do more than to draw together the scattered threads
of a collective experience, to correlate wandering
truisms, and to place in connexion with one another
considerations which are apt to present themselves
haphazard and in isolation.

It is a modern fashion to disparage Vergil. In
the eighteenth century his supremacy still stood not
only unshaken but unchallenged. In the century that
followed many causes operated together to lessen the
esteem in which he had been so long held. It was
the era of a criticism from which, in literature as in
everything else, no accepted opinion was exempt, no
accredited reputation safe. The increased diffusion

of Greek studies created an atmosphere unfavourable
to the appreciation of a literature so dependent and
so unoriginative as the Latin. Vergil had made the
mistake of not being Homer—just as all the Romans
made the mistake of not being the Greeks. It became
an affectation of the new Hellenism to slight him and to
ignore him. His reputation was, moreover, adversely
affected by *a priori* theories of the 'natural' character
of poetry—theories which at the beginning of the
nineteenth century had a wide vogue among con-
tinental critics. And in general it was felt that the
length and breadth of Vergil's influence in the world
had been out of all proportion to his genius or per-
formance. It was sought to explain this influence by
causes which may be called accidental. Chief among
these were the political dominance of Rome, the ex-
tinction in Western Europe of Greek speech and study,
the Italian origin of the Renaissance, the affinity to
Latin of the principal European tongues. All these
circumstances had combined to make the influence
of Vergil greater than that of far greater poets.

His works were now subjected in detail to a
vigorous and unsympathetic criticism. Their imita-
tive character was unduly emphasized. Little inquiry
was made into the true nature of artistic imitation ;
and they were condemned in the lump on an indictment which would lie against two-thirds of the best
modern poetry. The *Eclogues* were especially
assailed. Here Vergil had brushed the bloom and
freshness from a species of poetry the most simple
and natural and engaging. Claiming descent from
Theocritus, he had become the father of a long line

of bastard poetry; and among his progeny it might
be vainly debated whether the palm for frigidity
belonged to Calpurnius, to Mantuan, to Philips, to
Pope or to Collins. The *Aeneid* was an epic wholly
wanting in the first essential of that species of poetry,
epical *élan*. It had no joy in it of ' eventful living '.
Its gods were ghosts, its men milksops. At its best
it was elegy, at its worst kid-glove epic unashamed.
By a malicious paradox the *Georgics* were proclaimed
as Vergil's greatest achievement. But even here we
were not spared the picture of an incongruously
elegant Philosophy wandering disconsolate in the
world of the market-gardener and the veterinary
surgeon. His ' style' was conceded to Vergil, his
style and his rhythmical grandeur. But take from
him these, and what do you leave him?

We *cannot*, of course, take away these things. It
is false to think of poetry as *having* qualities. It *is*
its qualities. Vergil's ' style' is less a property than
a temper. It is ethical. It is a part of the whole
tissue of his poetry and his mind.

Of the criticism of his poetry as a whole which
I have just outlined it is obvious that a great part is,
in its general character, both exaggerated and perverse. Yet it contains elements of truth which it
would be both idle and injudicious to ignore. It
represents a very natural reaction; and, if we are
to try and judge Vergil truly, we must, I think,
go some way with this reaction. I will say at
once how far I am prepared to go with it. I will
go with it so far as to be ready to admit of each
of Vergil's three great works that it is, as it stands,

a failure.   In the *Eclogues* Vergil essays, I think, an
impossible *form*.   In the *Georgics* he has taken an
impossible subject-matter ; and the very perfection,
technically, of this work only serves to deepen the
sense of his failure.   The *Aeneid* has come down
to us unfinished.   The *Aeneid* also is a failure—
but let me add at once that it succeeds most precisely where it fails most : that just where it falls
short of being what Vergil meant it to be it begins
to be greatest and most truly Vergilian.   I will explain what I mean.   Vergil intended to devote three
more years to the *Aeneid*.   I am not sure that he
would have made it better.   At his death he ordered
it to be burnt.   I do not think that what troubled
him was the ' pathetic half-lines', the unpruned
diction, the makeshift joins and transitions.   It was
rather a defect in the whole work—a far-reaching
contradiction between conception and execution.
Conington, speaking of the fourth book of the
Aeneid, says that Vergil, in his treatment there of
the character of Dido, ' struck the chord of modern
passion, and it vibrated *more powerfully than the
minstrel himself expected.*'   That is true ; and that
was the trouble.   And it is a trouble which in various
ways infects the whole *Aeneid*.   Vergil is for ever in
the *Aeneid* being carried out of his own intention.
He is for ever being borne whither he would not by
a spirit of which the processes elude and the end
startles.   He is always left standing surprised before
some unplanned consummation, before some result
different from that calculated—and greater.   And it
is just because Vergil is always being thus drawn

away into the negation of his own rules that the
Aeneid is always just about to pass into the greatest
imaginative work of antiquity. Let me illustrate.

I will take first Vergil's hero. Some one has said
prettily that the history of Greece begins with Achilles
and ends with Alexander. We all of us, in any case,
like our heroes young. It is hot blood makes epic :
and Achilles is irresistible. There is no man who
has not felt sometimes, as Alexander felt always,
that he would like to be Achilles. But did ever man
wish to be Aeneas? One had as lief be Pompey—
' that most stiff and starched of artificial great men.'
It is not merely that Aeneas is so utterly middle-
aged. Ulysses (though I am not sure that the
Greeks ever quite forgave him for it) is middle-aged.
But Ulysses is still so fine a fighter, so fine a rascal,
of so fresh a sentimentality, still so apt for impossible
adventures, that he stands outside all laws of epic.
He is still young and alive by that law which is
as old as Solon and the wise Egyptian : ' O Solon,
Solon, you Greeks are always boys.' Contrast
Ulysses on his raft with the shipwrecked Aeneas in
the first book of the *Aeneid*! Aeneas never in his
life, one feels, tasted gladly the sea-salt on his lips,
nor felt the winds upon his face—or he felt them very
wearily and vaguely and humbly. If Vergil wished—
and I fear that he did—to give us an epic with an
epical hero, then Aeneas is undoubtedly, if I may
be allowed a homely phrase, *the wrong man in the
wrong place*. But as soon as we distinguish—and
everywhere in the *Aeneid* we must, I believe, so
distinguish—between what Vergil deliberately set

himself to do and that towards which nature, or
genius, obscurely directed him—here and elsewhere
our difficulties tend to disappear. Vergil set before
himself a Ulysses, perhaps even an Achilles. Nature
set before him a St. Louis—a crusading knight and
a '*holy* war'. In the issue he hovers between the
two conceptions—and fails. Yet there emerges from
the failure something greater, at any rate in hope
and suggestion, than any epical success : an ideal
and mystical figure standing outside time and place,
that seems to be now Aeneas, now Rome, now the
soul of Man setting forth doubtfully on the pilgrimage of a dimly descried eternal glory.

Let us turn to Dido. Vergil set himself to give
us a queen of tragedy. Clearly he worked at Dido
and Anna with his eye on Phaedra and the Nurse
in Euripides' *Hippolytus*. He meant to give us
a story of ὕβρις and the inevitable ἄτη that follows
upon it. The book is conceived throughout in the
spirit of Athenian drama [1] : and it is tragic in form
as well as in conception. Yet into the execution of
it there has crept something alien to the tragic
manner. There were never such tears for any
heroine of Attic tragedy as Augustine—and not he
alone—shed over Dido. And she was never meant
to deserve them! She was meant to be in the
wrong. How otherwise could Aeneas be in the
right? If we wish to know what Vergil meant by
Dido we must look at Anna. There are latent in
Dido all the faults that are patent in Anna.

---

[1] See the remarks of Nettleship in his essay upon the *Aeneid*,
Lectures and Essays, vol. i.

Id cinerem aut manes credis curare sepultos ?
says Anna to Dido.[1]

Scilicet is superis labor est, ea cura quietos
sollicitat.

says Dido to Aeneas.[2]   In both the same cynical
Epicureanism, the same revolt against life, the same
ὕβρις. They are true sisters, and Vergil means us
to know it : yet he ends himself by refusing to
believe it. He lets Aeneas slink away like a thief
in the grey of dawn : the holy Roman Empire goes
with him dishonoured and ashamed. One might
almost think that the poet was deliberately satirizing
an empire built, if ever one was, upon cant and self-
deception. It is Dido who remains holy and
glorified.

How has it all happened ? It has been wrought
by the operation of that spirit in every great poet
which is greater and stronger than himself : which
makes him pitiful when he would be stern, weak
when he would be terrible, romantic when he would
be classical, a Celt when he would be a Roman.
For there it is ! We ask, how has it all happened ?
Well, listen to this :

' Thou Sun, that dost bathe in fire all the works
of the world, and thou, Juno, that art privy to my
love and canst unlock its riddle, and Hecate unto
whom by the cross-roads there is wailing o' nights
through the cities, and all Avenging Angels—and
gods of dying Elissa . . .'[3]

How has *that* happened ? Where does it come
from ? Did any Roman write that ? Did any Roman

---

[1] *Aen.* iv. 34.   [2] *Aen.* iv. 379-80.   [3] *Aen.* iv. 607-10.

build that tremendous climax? I could believe it of Browning, who, in Guido's last appeal, hits a like effect:

> Abbate, Cardinal, Christ, Maria, God,
> Pompilia—will you let them murder me?

But it is hard to believe it of any Roman, save that it is there.

Take, again, Vergil's description of Dido's desolation after the failure of her last appeal to Aeneas [1] In the shrine of Sychaeus she hears strange voices, and Sychaeus himself seems to call her. Above the calling of her dead husband there sounds the incongruous hooting of owls, and withal there ring in her ears the prophecies of olden prophets. She dreams that she is some Maenad whom Aeneas drives before him in frenzy, 'and for ever she seems to be being left alone, to be setting forth ever upon some endless uncompanioned pilgrimage, and ever where no soul is to be seeking her Tyrians.' To say that there is nothing else like that in Roman poetry is to speak idly: for there is nothing else like it—so profound in psychology, so romantically mystical, so subtly overpowering—in all literature.

Consider once more the setting of natural scenery which Vergil gives to the consummation of Dido's sin with Aeneas. [2] The heaven thunders in uncertain tumult. Cloud and hail mingle. The streams tumble down the hillside. Earth and the goddess of wedlock give their sign. Fires flash from end to end of the 'guilty air'. The wailing of nymphs is

---

[1] *Aen.* iv. 457-68.   [2] *Aen.* iv. 160-8.

heard on the mountain heights. 'Such was the day', says Vergil, 'that began for Dido death and sin.'

Where does it all come from? From a source past tracing. Somewhere far back in time, before the name of Rome had travelled outside Latium, before Allia and Brennus, in some village camp at the foot of the Alps some rough Celtic warrior lay down with an unwilling Italian bride and begat without knowing it to a generation infinitely distant— Vergil! begat these strange spiritual contradictions, this epic failure, begat a spirit for ever over-mastered by purposes deeper than its own, for ever carried beyond the rules of its art to the edge of triumphs grander than any dream of Greece.

Vergil came to Rome from the other side of the Po; and the Po did not flow from the Alps to the Adriatic for nothing. The Transpadanes did not live where they did just to be like other Italians. Their country was familiarly spoken of as 'Gallia Togata'. But the men themselves were least of all the Italian dependencies a 'togate' race. We know them pretty well from the poetry of Catullus and his school. They were before all things a passionate race. They had two businesses in life—love and hate; and they plied either in a fashion reckless, unscrupulous, and often foul. They hated Rome and the Roman imperial idea. They hated Caesar, and they made him feel it in bitter lampoons by which Caesar is said to have thought himself disgraced for ever. They hated Roman poetry. They wanted a poetry of their own. And they had it. There was probably more of poetry as we conceive it, pure poetry, in Cisalpine Gaul, than in all the rest of the Roman Empire taken together. It was a poetry of revolt—these Transpadanes would not put their hearts to school. But it was poetry of a great and fierce quality, poignant and compelling.

It was in this air of revolt that Vergil first drew breath. This poet whom we regard as so typically Roman is half a Celt. And here lies, perhaps, the secret of his greatness, and, if one may still speak of such a thing, of his failure. In his poetry we have the first appearance in literature—in literature of any real depth and compass—of the romantic spirit. This gives to his work a supreme interest in the history of the development of Poetry. And it gives to it not merely a supreme historical interest, but also a supreme spiritual interest. Or rather, what is of supreme spiritual interest is not so much this manifestation in Vergil of the Celtic, or romantic, element as the conflict in him between this spirit and the other. And in fact his poetry, not merely here but everywhere, is essentially a poetry of spiritual conflict, of divided purpose, of unattained desire, of the stretching forth of hands in unrealized longing. It is by this precisely that it moves us more greatly than greater poetry.

We may study this conflict, if we will, in the story of Dido and Aeneas. But we may study it in many other aspects. We may go to Vergil's earliest period. We all know the conventional picture of Vergil's youth—the shy child ('the maiden') dreaming by the banks of the Mincius ('Minciades' Juvencus calls him), solemnizing his youthful soul with the shadows along the Mantuan hills. But there has come down to us under the name of Vergil a collection of short poems bearing the title *Catalepton*, 'Poems in Little'; and of none of these, save perhaps one, have we any good reason to suspect the authenticity: the learned labours of Dr. Birt have recently done much to confirm the tradition which ascribes them to Vergil. And if Vergil's they be, what a revelation are they! We see here nothing of the youthful saint, the recluse, the mystic, the divine aspirant; but a spirit undisciplined, reckless, fevered with passion, a Transpadane indeed, yet one in whom there is no softness, no dreaming, nothing of infinite desire. These poems take us in fact away from the quiet Mincius and from soft sleep in the grass to the fashionable life, with its gay enthusiasms and fierce animosities, of some Transpadane literary centre. There are some unpleasant pieces of invective; and everywhere passion, conflict, revolt, worldliness. Out of all this was born the Vergil whom we know. In 'mortal moral strife' came to him that revelation which he has to offer to us.

Look again at what we call his philosophy—what we should more appropriately call his religious creed. We often say of him quite blithely that he is an Epicurean in the *Eclogues* and *Georgics*, and a Stoic in the *Aeneid*. We are so accustomed to saying it that it never seems to startle us as it should. It never seems to imply anything of stress and striving, of wrestling with God to know his name. Yet these are not idle distinctions—or they were

not. It would startle us to learn that Milton was
a Puritan in *Paradise Lost* and a Catholic in *Paradise
Regained*. We should feel that here was a fact of
supreme importance for criticism. Well, the man
who wrote the *Aeneid* is a man who has undergone
a conversion not much dissimilar to that which I am
supposing for Milton. The 'walls of the world' have
fallen down before him.[1] He has felt the Spirit
breathing upon the gross clay of the material
universe—

totamque infusa per artus
mens agitat molem[2];—

he is a different man and a different poet.

The relation of Poetry to Philosophy is still a
mystery that neither poet nor philosopher can solve
for us. Plato speaks somewhere of a παλαιὸν νεῖκος,
an 'ancient conflict', between poet and philosopher.
This 'ancient conflict', which troubled the 'seraphic
soul' of Plato, had very early indeed disturbed and
perplexed Vergil.

'Away, hollow bombast of the rhetoricians, and
words waxed gross on other dews than those of
Grecian eloquence. Away, Silius, Tarquitius, Varro,
tribe of pedants fat and greasy; away hollow tinkling
of light-minded youth. You also, Sextus Sabinus, dear
heart, farewell. O now farewell, all lovely and pleasant
friends. I am setting sail for the haven of happiness,
I am making straight course to the wisdom of noble
Siron. I would fain wrest my life from all cares.
Begone, Muses, you too begone and farewell, pleasant

---

[1] Lucretius, iii. 16–17 *moenia mundi discedunt.*
[2] *Aen.* vi. 726–7.

Muses : for pleasant you were in all truth. And yet now and again visit my pages : but only now and again and but shyly.'

That is from the *Catalepton*; and it belongs perhaps to Vergil's seventeenth year. He bids farewell, you will notice, to poetry and to romance, and to the two sciences which dogged always the footsteps of Latin poetry, scholarship and rhetoric. He bids farewell to poetry and romance. He is embarked for ' the haven of happiness '. He has had enough of the disease of sensibility. He would fain bring his soul to port in philosophy. Some twenty years later, in the closing passage of the second book of the *Georgics*, he returns to the theme of the relation of poetry to philosophy. It is the well-known passage [1] which begins

Me vero primum dulces ante omnia Musae ;

and in those opening words it is, I think, not over fanciful to suppose that Vergil consciously recalled the

dulces Camenae, nam fatebimur verum,
dulces fuistis

of the early *Catalepton* poem. What has happened in the twenty years between the one piece and the other ? Let us hear Vergil himself :

' Me may the Muses take for their priest, the pleasant Muses, whose holy emblems I bear, the wound of whose love is in my heart. As their scholar let me learn the goings of the starry heaven, the manifold travail of the sun and the moon's labour : whence comes the shock of earthquake, under what

[1] *Geog.* ii. 475 sqq.

impulsion the deep seas rise in wrath beyond their broken barriers and anon sink back into their old peace : wherefore the suns in winter make such ado to dip themselves in Ocean, and what cross-purpose meets the nights that they tarry so long.'

These lines may be regarded as Vergil's hesitant 'Prayer for the Union of Poetry and Philosophy'. I say a hesitant prayer ; and it is, for he goes on

' But if the lively current of the blood stand frozen about my heart in such sort that I may not come nigh unto this philosophy, then be my pleasure the country-side and the streams that water the valleys. May I love rivers and woodland, and be fame far from me.'

Then he speaks of himself side by side with Rome's greatest philosophic poet :

' Blessed is he who has won to the knowledge of nature, who has put in subjection under his feet all fear and fate inexorable and the outcry of the greedy grave. Yet happy he also who is the friend of the gods of the countryside, Pan and old Silvanus and the sisterhood of the nymphs.'

The theme here is the same as that in the seventh poem of the *Catalepton*, but viewed somewhat differently. There he was ready to abandon poetry for philosophy. Here he contemplates some possible union of the two. But doubtfully ; and if one of them must be resigned it is to be philosophy. His last word upon the subject comes to us on the report of others from the last year of his life. We are told by Vergil's biographer that he intended, at the time when he died, to give three years to the revision of the *Aeneid* and to *devote the rest of his life to philo-*

sophy. He counted himself not to have attained.
It is a strange story; but it comes to us upon good
authority, and the more closely we study Vergil the
more likely, I fancy, shall we be to think it true.
His last word to us is that in philosophy, which is
everything, he knows nothing; and that in poetry
he no longer believes, least of all in his own. We
may burn the *Aeneid*.

Yet the *Aeneid* is great just for the reason for
which Vergil wished to burn it—just because Vergil
has not attained, just because the poem carries with
it the infection of an unsatisfied soul. Vergil is
never wholly at home with himself. His poetry
is never quite a unity. He essays a warrior, and
achieves—or nearly—a visionary. He pictures a
city, and it seems to melt into a Church. He nerves
himself to be terrible and pitiless to a woman's sin :
yet, like his own Aeneas,[1] and more truly,

> prosequitur lacrimans longe et miseratur euntem.

He tries to depict in Turnus lawless and ungoverned
passion bent upon its proper destruction ; and he
gives us a character whom some have taken for the
true hero of the *Aeneid*. He throws himself in an
ardour of passionate devotion upon the philosophy
of Lucretius ; and then shrinks back from the iron
laws whose presence he has invoked. Always something breaks in upon his resolution. Always, when
he sees the light, he sighs.

There is this conflict, then, in all his poetry, this

[1] *Aen.* vi. 476.

spiritual division, this quarrel with itself of a mystical
and romantic genius working unsatisfied within the
limits of a formal classicism, never quite confident,
never wholly efficient. It is because of this that
Vergil has been the subject of judgements so diverse ;
that he has seemed to some hardly a poet at all, to
others a prophet, a revealer, a priest of the innermost
mystery of the soul. I have mentioned his influence
upon religious thought. The single name of Dante
is enough. Dante likens Vergil in his religion to one
who bears a torch from which he himself derives no
light but which gives light to those that follow after
him. The figure is pitched to mediaeval standards.
I would prefer to say quite simply that Vergil in his
religion, as in everything else, stands always on the
brink of a revelation which he never consummates.
As in Aeneas, as in Dido—so here, he is always
groping his way obscurely towards effects that fail.
We all know how to Dante he seemed a prophet of
the Christian Messiah. Yet we know also how he
lent his genius to a crude apotheosis of Augustus.
Here is the old contradiction and division. Vergil
lived in a tired world : ' us upon whom are come the
ends of the ages '—that text is, as it were, written
over the whole literature of the period. But it is a
world stirred, however doubtfully, from one end of it
to the other, by a great expectancy. Before Christ
the weary West had heard and caught up from the
East a mystical voice—' Maranatha '. The East
understood. The West awaited an interpreter. To
Vergil was given that high office. ' Draw nigh—
the times are ready—O now draw nigh, to the worship

of the great world, child of the gods most loved,
mighty seed of Jupiter.' So he apostrophizes[1] in
language of passionate expectancy some mysterious
Redeemer unguessed at ; and he paints for us the
splendour and holiness of the renewed and redeemed
world in language which seems to answer the cry of
the heart in all ages for some peace of God which
passes understanding. It is hard to believe that it
is the same poet who in the *Georgics* asks Augustus
whether he will be still a god of the earth, giving
man the fruits in their seasons, or a god of sea and
seamen, or a constellation in the heavens, or even
one of the lords of Hell. Just as in depicting Aeneas
he stands irresolute between an Achilles and a
St. Louis, so here, in his prophecy of a saviour of
the world, he hovers ineffectually, I will not say
between Christ and Caesar, but between an ideal
humanity, the vision of which alone is life to men
and nations, and a prince of this world not among
the noblest, not made for love, earthly, unspiritual.

The same hesitancy meets us, under a somewhat
different aspect, when we contemplate the gods and
goddesses who wander in such stately ineffectiveness
across the pages of the *Aeneid*.[2] Of these I will say
but a word or two—which I would wish to be interpreted as in the nature of a hurried footnote (for the
sands in my hour-glass have run very low) to what
I have just said. It is charged against Vergil that
he has merely ' taken over ' the old Homeric mytho-

---

[1] *Ecl.* iv. 46-7.
[2] I am indebted in what follows to Heinze, *Virgil's Epische Technik,*[1]
pp. 284 sqq.

logy—an epic machinery incongruous and out of
date : that these are the same gods and goddesses
as those of Homer—only less interesting. That
is not true. In a sense they are less interesting.
They are, that is to say, less like men and women.
They have less individual personality. Only one
of them, in fact—Jupiter—has a real personality at
all ; and it is not the personality of the Homeric
Zeus. The Homeric Zeus is just like the rest of
Homer's gods and goddesses—only stronger. He is
primus inter pares, and he rules Olympus merely by
his superior strength, by brute force, as it were.
And he, like the rest of them, is subject to Fate.
But the Jupiter of Vergil is *Omnipotens*, he is *hominum rerumque aeterna potestas*, and the Fates are
spoken of as *belonging to him* (*fata Iovis*). Here
as everywhere Vergil is just passing—and just not
passing—from the traditional, the formal, the con-
ditioned, into a free spiritual world. Jupiter is still
to some extent the old Homeric Zeus. Yet again
and again Vergil uses of him language such as is
never used—never could be used—by Homer of
Zeus, and such as might be applied with perfect
propriety to the god of a monotheistic system. The
other gods and goddesses are merely episodic ; and
Vergil deliberately empties them of all personality.
They become mere shadowy ministers, or instru-
ments, of the one supreme Will.

How does this supreme Will execute its purposes ?
It sends out its messengers. What do they effect ?
They effect nothing at all. Mercury goes to Carthage.
He is bidden to conciliate the Tyrians to the Trojans.

How does he do it ?   Vergil never tells us.

> Ponuntque ferocia Poeni
> corda volente deo : in primis regina quietum
> accipit in Teucros animum.[1]

That is all he says.   Mercury is a mere symbol.
It would all happen without him.   Even where the
symbolism is made more concrete it is the same.
An exchange is effected between Cupid and Ascanius.
Cupid takes the place of Ascanius, and lies on Dido's
breast.[2]   But so careless is Vergil of his mythological
machinery that Cupid remains Ascanius to the end
of the story.   Vergil never troubles to effect the
exchange back.   These things are symbol and
ornament.   What we are offered always is not
a psychological situation created by supernatural
agency, but a self-created psychological situation
accompanied by, and symbolized, sometimes more,
sometimes less, vividly by supernatural agency.   Of
every effect of divine intervention in the *Aeneid* we
may ask the question which, in the ninth book,[3]
Nisus asks of Euryalus :

> Dine hunc ardorem mentibus addunt,
> Euryale, an sua cuique deus fit dira cupido ?

—is this some god of mythology, or the mystery of
our own souls ?   That is the question which Vergil
is always asking himself—and never answering.
This priest of the soul of man is never quite assured.
This interpreter of the heavenly mysteries cannot
yet tell us certainly whether God is a spirit or whether
heaven is still as Homer made it.

[1] *Aen.* i. 302-4.   [2] *Aen.* i. 657-722.   [3] *Aen.* ix. 184-5.

It is a great thing that he asks at all the questions which he never answers. And he does this everywhere, in religion, in life, and in his art. Everywhere he sees visions—which he cannot hold. He is for ever lifting the veil of the romance of life—and it falls again. He is for ever about to give us something greater in art than the rest of antiquity can show—and for ever just missing the supreme effect. Yet his failure is of the order which sanctifies. It sanctifies as Aeneas is sanctified when he reaches out his arms to clasp the ghost of Creusa amid the burning of Troy,[1] or the wraith of Anchises in the Elysian fields.[2] It is the melancholy sanctification of all those who, in fire or darkness, see and know for their own and throw themselves with frustrated longing upon something that is of another and nobler and purer world—

Ter conatus ibi collo dare bracchia circum,
ter frustra comprensa manus effugit imago,
par levibus ventis volucrique simillima somno.

[1] *Aen.* ii. 792–5.   [2] *Aen.* vi. 679–702.

OVID AND ROMANCE

By S. G. Owen

Though he did not possess the dignity of Virgil or the conciseness of Horace, if popularity is a true test of merit, Ovid holds no mean place of honour among the Roman poets. He was read eagerly in his lifetime, and has been read no less eagerly ever since. If imagination, descriptive power, and lucidity of style count for anything in letters, Ovid was a great man of letters. His works fall into three divisions : love poems, narrative pieces, and the melancholy productions in which he laments in exquisite verse the sorrows of the cruel banishment that embittered the close of his life.

In love poetry he excelled. 'I am love's professor'[1] he slyly said, at the time when he was the accepted poet of fashionable Rome. The *Amores*, his earliest production, are light and trivial love poems, delicate in texture but without profound passion or deep feeling, except in the case of the elegy on the death of his fellow poet Tibullus (*Am.* iii. 9). In the *Ars Amatoria*, his most audacious work, he deals ironically with his subject. The poem is almost a satire upon woman, less trenchant than Juvenal's sixth satire, but not less effective. This masterpiece

---

[1] *A. A.* i. 17 'ego sum praeceptor amoris'.

contains brilliant episodes, which first reveal the poet's supreme power of narrative. In the *Heroides*, supposed letters from renowned legendary ladies to their absent lords, he revels in psychological analysis of feeling, pique, pride, affection, despair, the whole being executed with faultless skill of composition, which had been acquired when he studied rhetoric as a young man in the school of the distinguished teacher of rhetoric Porcius Latro, under whose guidance, according to the elder Seneca, he devoted himself to the emotional rather than the argumentative side of rhetoric.[1]

As Ovid grew older he aimed higher. He knew his own limitations, and was too sensible to court failure by attempting to write epic, a task beyond his powers. But being fully conscious of his own abundant faculty for narrative, he set about the composition of the *Metamorphoses*, a poem in fifteen books, in which are described all the legends concerning miraculous transformations of human beings into animals, birds, or other objects, which sort of miracles played no small part in ancient mythology. The subject had been partially treated before by the early Alexandrine poet Boios, a mysterious personage who, under the name of a Delphian priestess Boio, wrote a poem (*Ornithogonia*) recounting the origins of different birds from men ; by Nicander of Colophon, in the second century B.C., who wrote a poem in five books on changes of shape (ἑτεροιούμενα) ; and by the

---

[1] Senec. *Contr*. ii. 2. 12 'declamabat autem Naso raro controversias et non nisi ethicas ; libentius dicebat suasorias. Molesta illi erat omnis argumentatio'.

Greek poet Parthenius of Nicaea, a contemporary of
Ovid, who composed a *Metamorphoses*, from which
title Ovid probably borrowed the name of his work.
These sources, and others, such as the *Hecale* of
Callimachus, were used by Ovid with freedom and
discretion, just as he has himself been used by later
poets. But it seems probable that his specific debt
to his predecessors was inconsiderable; outlines he
borrowed not details; though he did not invent his
stories, he told them with the inimitable grace of his
genius, with simplicity, vivacity, and eloquence. The
dull religious legends grew into poetry under his
hands; for he could not write otherwise than as
a poet. He said truly of himself:

Et quod temptabam dicere versus erat

(*Trist.* iv. 10. 26), which Pope paraphrased:

I lisped in numbers, for the numbers came.

The *Metamorphoses* is a veritable encyclopaedia of
legend. It must be read through to gain an adequate
idea of Ovid's marvellous versatility and narrative
skill. Its abundant material has supplied poets with
a rich storehouse of incidents and ideas, and of these
they have freely availed themselves. Thus Ovid
was justified in the proud prophecy with which he
concludes his vast work, foretelling that it will bring
to him immortality of fame that neither the anger of
heaven, nor fire, nor sword, nor time's ruin shall
destroy.[1]

[1] *Met.* xv. 871 ff.:

    Iamque opus exegi, quod nec Iovis ira nec ignis
    Nec poterit ferrum nec edax abolere vetustas. . . .
    . . . . . . perque omnia saecula fama,
    Siquid habent veri vatum praesagia, vivam.

The *Metamorphoses* is written in the stately hexa-
meter metre, the metre of the epic.   The rest of
Ovid's works are cast in elegiac couplets, the traditional verse of themes devoted to sorrow or love.
Of this metre Ovid is recognized to be the greatest
master, and, with daring innovation, in the *Fasti* he
ventured to divert it from its customary uses and to
employ it for narrative.   The *Fasti* is a calendar in
verse of the Roman year, describing the national and
religious festivals and other anniversaries; it is replete
with information about ceremonial, history, folk-lore,
and legend.   Like the *Metamorphoses* it has yielded
abundant matter for romance, such as the tale of
Arion, who

> Could humanise the creatures of the sea
> When men were monsters   (WORDSWORTH)

(*Fast.* ii. 83) the history of the outraged Lucrece
(*Fast.* ii. 791), the legend of the rape of Proserpine
by Pluto (*Fast.* iv. 417), and the account of the
humorous misadventure which befell Faunus (*Fast.*
ii. 331), which may have helped to suggest to
Chaucer the Reve's Tale.

In the fiftieth year of his life, having reached the
climax of literary and social success, Ovid was
banished by the Emperor Augustus for some unknown cause, apparently nearly affecting the honour
of the imperial house, though the improprieties of
the *Ars Amatoria* furnished the actual pretext.
The unfortunate poet was dispatched to live and die
at Tomi, near the modern Kustendji, south of the
mouth of the Danube on the Black Sea, and in that

dismal frontier outpost, besides writing the *Ibis*, an invective against an unnamed enemy, he composed and sent to Rome the *Tristia* and *Epistulae ex Ponto*, a melancholy series of poetical lamentations upon his exile, mixed with apologies vainly addressed to the inflexible emperor. Yet even in these poems of a broken man, the brilliancy of language and fancy, and the supple fertility with which he rings the changes on his unchanging subject show that exile itself could not stale or wither his genius.

Above all Roman poets Ovid was endowed with imagination. But his talent was not for epic or tragic poetry. He did as a fact write a tragedy on Medea, of which Quintilian remarks (*Inst. Orat.* x. 1. 98) that it shows how much he might have achieved in this line if he had been able to curb his luxuriance. The fact that it has not come down to us suggests that by general consent it was unsuccessful. Indeed, the natural bent of his genius did not concern itself with the inexorable working out of human destiny, and the study of mankind in situations of pity and terror. His mind moved in a wonderland created by his own warm fancy, in a world of romantic love and adventure, peopled with beings young and strong and beautiful. The everyday life of the gay society of his own time lives again in the airy sketches of his love poems. The outraged brides of the remote past, who form the subject of the *Heroides*, express their anguish and affection in language which proves that Ovid accurately understood the heart of woman. In the *Metamorphoses* and *Fasti* he invests the ancient legends with lifelike freshness. There is no spiritual

purpose or moral background.   He tells his stories
from mere romantic impulse : the gods and nymphs,
heroes, heroines, and peasants of the past become real
personages in his vivid verse.   And his romantic
sympathy extends beyond his personal creations to the
world of nature.   He loves the wild mountains, glens
and forests and cool caverns, the glassy streams and
lakes, the wide sea whether still or stormy, and the
islands which are scattered over its surface.   He has,
moreover, the genuine romantic love of detail.   When
the lad Phaethon is hurried in his wild course through
the sky by the horses of his father the sun-god which
he aspired to drive, and surveys the whole world on
fire beneath him, cities and nations perishing in ashes,
mountains and rivers burnt up, the names of all are
recounted in a long catalogue of strange poetic effec-
tiveness (*Met.* ii. 215 ff.).   A similar catalogue of the
places visited by Ceres in her world-wide search for
her lost daughter Proserpina is enriched with all a
poet's subtle luxuriance of telling epithets (*Fast.* iv.
467 ff.).   The hounds of the ill-fated Theban youth
Actaeon which tore their master to death, thirty-seven
in number each called by an appropriate name, are
enumerated in order to suggest the size of the pack,
and thus enhance the horror of the brutal scene
(*Met.* iii. 206 ff.).   The poet's opulent fancy lingers
over the names of the places past which Arethusa
sped in her flight from Alpheus, and of the mountains
and rivers visited by Medea in her winged chariot,
when she culled the drugs with which to restore the
aged Aeson to youth (*Met.* v. 607 ff., vii. 222 ff.).
The giant Polyphemus, singing the beauty of Galatea

fairer than white privet yet more treacherous than the waves, accumulates image upon image with which to compare her beauty; for a giant's store of similitudes must be gigantic (*Met.* xiii. 788 ff.). Of all Roman poets Ovid has the richest and most sensuous eye for colours, the red gold of the golden fleece or lion's mane (*Am.* ii. 11. 4, *Met.* x. 698), the orange red of cedar or Apollo's hair (*Trist.* iii. 1. 13, *Am.* i. 15. 35), the brown of storm-clouds (*Met.* v. 286), the yellow of the crocus (*Met.* iii. 509), the dusky hue of the mulberry (*Met.* iv. 160), the glassy-green of sea waves (*Met.* v. 48), and many more.

Such characteristics as these have endeared Ovid to romantic writers. Unity and regularity are the marks of classical composition; diversity and picturesqueness of romance. It was Ovid who, scorning the severity of classical style, gave free scope to his fertile imagination, and thus prepared the way for a new movement which drew its impulse from the qualities prominent in youth,—uncritical delight in the beauty of nature, and the emotions of joy and sorrow. His works were studied ardently throughout the Middle Ages, though the more pious looked with suspicion on the pagan legends because they savoured of idolatry. 'It is rank idolatry', says the twelfth-century Benedictine monk Conrad of Hirschau, 'that Ovid should state in the *Metamorphoses* that the nature of a rational creature was changed by the gods into that of a stone or beast or bird.'[1]

---

[1] Conrad of Hirschau flourished 1070-1150. See G. Schepss, *Conradi Hirschaugiensis Dialogus super auctores sive Didascalon*, Würtzburg, 1889, p. 66.

But monks were not all of Conrad's way of thinking ; and his works were translated early into the
vernacular languages, French, Italian, German.
A Byzantine Greek, Planudes, who lived at Constantinople in the latter half of the thirteenth
century, and combined the occupations of a monk
and a diplomatist, rendered into Greek in versions
which are still extant the whole of the *Heroides* and
Metamorphoses and the *Ars Amatoria* ; part of his
version of this latter poem has been found recently at
Naples and published by Schenkl.[1]   When the
humanists of the Renaissance discovered anew the
half-forgotten classical learning, the spirituality and
superstitious mysticism of the Middle Ages gave
place to a sensuous and artistic culture, and Ovid,
the least spiritual and most sensuous of the ancients,
became the poet of poets and painters, the dominant
influence in art.   His characters crowd the canvas
in all the galleries of Europe : his mythology predominates in the Italians Boccaccio and Ariosto
and in our English Chaucer and Gower.   With
Chaucer and Gower our national poetry proper
begins.   Both these writers drew from many
sources, especially the Anglo-French romances,
and Chaucer from the Italian Boccaccio ; but it was
to Ovid among the ancient poets that they chiefly
turned for inspiration.

Though Chaucer was slightly younger than his

---

[1] Palmer, Ovid's *Heroides*, ed. 2, p. xlvi; Lemaire's *Ovid*, vol. v,
containing Boissonade's memorable edition of Planudes' version of the
Metamorphoses ; H. Schenkl, Στρωματεῖς, Grazer Festgabe, Graz, 1909,
p. 105.

friend Gower, he led the way in writing poetry in the English tongue, and his success undoubtedly induced Gower to follow his example. · One of Chaucer's chief charms is his marvellous skill in narrative, which he manages with an ease and simplicity that suggests the manner of his master Ovid. For though Chaucer openly renders 'glory and honour to Mantuan Virgil',[1] his admiration for Ovid would seem to have been greater, since his knowledge of classical mythology is derived mainly from Ovid, whom he often mentions by name. In the introduction to the Man of Law's Prologue in the *Canterbury Tales*, after boasting that he has himself told more stories than Ovid 'made mention of', he implicitly acknowledges his obligation to the Roman, for the list that he gives of his stories reveals that Ovid was his principal source (Skeat, *Chaucer*, iv. 131).

The debt of Chaucer to Ovid is clearest in the poems composed before the *Canterbury Tales*. In the earliest work, *The Book of the Duchess* (1369), he derived from the *Metamorphoses* (xi. 410–748) the tale of Alcyone and her husband Ceyx; how Ceyx the king was drowned at sea, and how his body was brought by Morpheus the god of sleep in a dream to Alcyone, in order that from her dead husband's lips she might learn his death. In Ovid the faithful lovers are converted into kingfishers : in Chaucer the queen dies of grief, a climax more natural and more in harmony with later thought.

The idea of Chaucer's next work, *The House of Fame* (1384), was suggested partly by Ovid's

------

[1] *Legend of Good Women*, 924.

description of the House of Fame (*Met.* xii. 39 ff.).
The picture of the god of sleep ' with his thousand
sleepy sons' is borrowed from Ovid's description of
the god of sleep (*Met.* xi. 592–632). The pairs of
lovers passed in review, Phyllis and Demophoon,
Briseis and Achilles, Jason and Hypsipyle, Jason
and Medea, Hercules and Deianira, Theseus and
Ariadne, are the pairs of lovers that Ovid's *Heroides*
had already made famous.

It is the same with the *Legend of Good Women*
(1385), which immediately preceded the *Canterbury
Tales.* In the Prologue the transformation of the
queen Alcestis into a daisy was suggested by Ovid's
Clytie, who pined away for the love of the sun-god
and was changed into a sunflower, the flower which
turns constantly towards the sun, or by the nymph
Daphne, who was converted at her own prayer into
a bay-tree (*Prol.* 499 ; Ov. *Met.* iv. 269, i. 545).
Of the tales of 'dead ladies' unfortunate in their
love, which form the subject of the *Legend*, all
except that of Cleopatra are from Ovid. From the
Metamorphoses is taken the oriental tale of Thisbe
and her lover Pyramus, familiar to English readers
from Shakespeare's *Midsummer Night's Dream.*
This is almost the only story in Ovid of which no
source has been discovered ; Ovid himself says that
it is little known, 'haec vulgaris fabula non est'
(*Met.* iv. 53) : he may have picked it up from some
swarthy Syrian in the streets of cosmopolitan Rome,
or even have invented it (*Legend* ii ; Ov. *Met.* iv.
53–166). From the *Metamorphoses* is taken the
story of Procne and her unfortunate sister Philomela,

whom the wicked king Tereus immured in a castle, having deprived her of speech by cutting out her tongue. Chaucer, who was no lover of horrors, forbore to complete the ghastly tragedy, in the details of which the Roman poet revelled, how Procne killed her son Itys and served him up for food to his father Tereus, and how Procne was changed into a swallow, Philomela into a nightingale, and Tereus into a hoopoe (*Legend* vii; Ov. *Met.* vi. 424 ff.). The story of Ariadne deserted by Theseus is composite: the first part is derived from the *Metamorphoses* (*Legend* vi. 1–2166; *Met.* vii. 456 ff., viii. 6 ff.), the second from the Tenth Epistle of the *Heroides*, to which authority Chaucer expressly appeals :

What shall I telle more her compleining ?
Hit is so long, hit were an hevy thing.
In her epistle Naso telleth all. (*Legend* vi. 2218.)

The story of Jason and Medea is also composite, taken partly from the *Heroides* and partly from the *Metamorphoses* (*Legend* iv, *Her.* xii, and *Met.* vii). From the *Heroides* are derived the legends of Hypsipyle, Phyllis and Hypermnestra, and part of that of Dido (*Legend* iv, *Her.* vi ; *Legend* viii, *Her.* ii and xiv; *Legend* iii, *Her.* vii).

The *Canterbury Tales* owe much to Ovid. In the Knight's Tale the paintings in the temple of Diana, 'woful Calistopee,' the Callisto of the *Fasti* (*Knight's Tale* 2056 ; *Fast.* ii. 153), Daphne, Actaeon, Atalanta, and Meleager are from Ovid (*Knight's Tale*, 2062 ff. ; *Met.* i. 452 ff., iii. 138 ff., viii. 260 ff.).

In the *Monk's Tale*, the death of Hercules brought
about by the fatal gift of the shirt of Nessus
stained with the blood of the dying centaur, which
was sent to the faithless hero by his wife Deianira,
though based immediately on Boethius, is from
Ovid (*Monk's Tale*, 3285 ff.; Boeth. *Cons. Phil.*
iv. 7; Ov. *Met.* ix. 134 ff. and *Her.* ix).

The Manciple's Tale of the Crow is taken from
the *Metamorphoses* (ii. 531 ff.). Ovid relates that
Phoebus the god of archery and healing loved the
maiden Coronis, and set his attendant bird the
raven (*corvus*), or, as Chaucer has it, the crow, to
watch over her, and that she yielded to infidelity,
and her indiscretion was reported by the raven to
his master Phoebus, who in anger slew Coronis,
and turned the colour of the raven, originally white,
to black, because he had been apprised by that bird
of his own dishonour.   As the story is exceptionally
well told by Ovid, certainly better than by his
English translators, and as it has been dignified by
Chaucer with a place in the *Canterbury Tales*, I have
ventured to translate it, that those who are familiar
with Chaucer may contrast the peculiarities of the
original upon which he built.

> Of all fair ladies wide Thessalia bare
> Coronis of Larissa was most fair ;
> A maid of gracious life and sweet renown
> She dwelt the glory of Larissa town ;
> So Phoebus loved and took her for his mate,
> Phoebus the lord of Delphi's hallowed state,
> And set to watch and keep her safe from ill
> His bird the raven that performs his will.

Alas! the bird with ever-watchful eye
Perceived her sin, and sped his flight on high,
Inexorable informer, to his lord,
And of Coronis' frailty brought him word.
When the god lover learned the story dread,
His crown of bay leaves tumbled from his head,
He dropped his lyre, his visage was transformed,
His cheek grew pale, and for revenge he stormed;
He seized his quiver, and his bow he bent,
And one inevitable arrow sent,
Which pierced the breast that was his sole delight.
Coronis groaned and, fallen in evil plight,
Drew forth the deadly steel, while streams of
    blood
Bathed her white limbs about with scarlet flood.
So from her veins she yielded forth her breath,
And all her body felt the frost of death.
His cruel vengeance now alas! too late
The god upbraids, and views himself with hate
Because he listened, and with anger burned;
He hates the bird from whom the offence he learned;
He hates his bow, and hates the hand that drew
The string, and hates the reckless shafts that slew.
Too late he clasps her lifeless to his heart,
And strives to baffle death with healing art.
But vain his effort: soon the pyre is raised
That must devour those limbs he oft had praised.
Silent he groans (high gods disdain to shed
Warm tears of pity for the sorrowful dead)
So groans the mother cow when sad, wide-eyed,
She sees her calf dragged rudely from her side,
And from the butcher's ear with noisy blow
The hammer swings, and lays the victim low.
But thankless perfumes now the god must place
Upon her form, and give the last embrace,
And pay the last sad seemly obsequies
To her that dead by death unseemly lies.

Next on the raven looking for reward,
Because she spoke the truth and kept good guard,
He turns his vengeance; black are now her wings,
Numbered no more among white birds she sings;
The mischief to her tell-tale tongue is due,
And so the white is turned to sable hue.

The raven, which Chaucer calls the crow, was associated with Phoebus the god of augury, because
soothsayers foretold the future from its flight.[1]
Chaucer expands the story, dwelling on the jealousy
of Phoebus, and remarks that to confine a woman
against her will is as vain labour as to put a bird in
a cage, for 'although the cage of gold be never so gay'
'the bird would liefer be' at liberty 'in a forest'.

The Lover's Confession or *Confessio Amantis* of
Gower, which was first completed in 1390, is a
miscellany of stories in verse of which the general
theme is love. The tales are told with force and
picturesqueness, and many come from Ovid, chiefly
from the *Metamorphoses*, though the *Heroides*,
Fasti, and *Tristia* have also been laid under contribution. Thus in Book I we read of the hunter
Actaeon, who seeing Diana and her nymphs bathing
was transformed into a stag and torn to pieces by

---

[1] Haupt on Ov. *Met.* ii. 544. The story is translated from *Met.* ii.
542-632, with the omission of 548-98, in which lines Ovid inserts into
the middle of the narrative the kindred story of an inquisitive maiden
who was transformed by Minerva into a crow (*cornix*). I have
transferred lines 540-1 to the end of the passage, where they fit in better
in the English. The idea that it was unbecoming in the gods to yield
to the human emotion of weeping, repeated in *Fast.* iv. 521 'neque enim
lacrimare deorum est,' is found in Euripides, *Hippolytus* 1396 ὁρῶ· κατ'
ὄσσων δ' οὐ θέμις βαλεῖν δάκρυ, 'I see, but from my eyes may shed no tear,'
said by Artemis.

his own hounds; of the slaying by Perseus of the
Gorgons, the sight of whose faces turned all men to
stone ; of Narcissus, who had such pride that he held
no woman worthy of his love, but at last, seeing his
own face reflected in water, became enamoured of it
and in vain despair struck himself against a rock
and died, and from his dead body sprang the flower.[1]
In Book II we read of the love of the giant Polyphemus for Galatea, and the story of Deianira and
the death of Hercules.[2] In Book III we read of the
guilty passion of Canace for her brother Macareus ;
in this case the suppression of some of Ovid's details
does credit to the delicacy of Gower's mind. We
read also of the blind prophet Tiresias ; of Phoebus
and Coronis, the subject of Chaucer's Manciple's Tale;
of the tell-tale nymph Lara, called by Gower Laar,
whose tongue was cut out because she gossiped
about Jupiter; of Pyramus and Thisbe, in which
story Gower follows Ovid less closely than Chaucer
did in the *Legend of Good Women* ; also of the love
of Phoebus for Daphne, who was transformed into
a bay-tree, or as Gower puts it a ' lorer tre '.[3] In
Book IV we read of Aeneas and Dido, Ulysses and
Penelope, Pygmalion and the statue, of Iphis transformed from a woman into a man, of Phyllis and

[1] *Conf. Am.* i. 338 ff., *Met.* iii. 138 ff. ; *Conf. Am.* i. 385 ff., *Met.* iv.
772 ff. ; *Conf. Am.* i. 2254 ff., *Met.* iii. 402 ff.

[2] *Conf. Am.* ii. 97 ff., *Met.* xiii. 750 ff. ; *Conf. Am.* ii. 2145 ff., *Met.*
ix. 101 ff., *Heroid.* ix.

[3] *Conf. Am.* iii. 143 ff., *Heroid.* xi ; *Conf. Am.* iii. 731 ff., *Met.* iii.
316 ff. ; *Conf. Am.* iii. 783 ff., *Met.* ii. 542 ff. ; *Conf. Am.* ii. 818 ff.,
Fast. ii. 585 ff. (The name of the nymph in Ovid is Lara, which appears
later as Lala, showing that the etymology is from λαλεῖν.) *Conf. Am.*
ii. 1331 ff., *Met.* iv. 55 ff.; *Conf. Am.* ii. 1685 ff., *Met.* i. 453 ff.

Demophoon, of Phaethon driving the chariot of the sun, of Laodamia and her gallant husband Protesilaus, who was the first of the Greek invaders to land on the coast of Troy and was killed in fulfilment of an oracle of which he knew the purport, of the fight between Hercules and the river-god Achelous, of Ceyx and Alcyone, which finely told story contains a beautiful description of the Cave of Sleep, where the sun never shines,

> So that no man may know aright,
> The point between the day and night.

We have too the stories of Argus and Io, and of Iphis and Anaxarete.[1] In Book V we read of Midas the king of Phrygia, who restored Silenus to Bacchus, of the detection by Vulcan of the intrigue between Mars and Venus, of Medea, of the punishment of Echo, of Procne, Philomela and Tereus, whose story had already been told by Chaucer in the *Legend of Good Women*, of Cornix, transformed into a crow, pursued by Neptune, of Callisto, whom Gower calls Calistona, of Leucothoe, and of the deception practised on Faunus by Hercules and Omphale.[2]

---

[1] *Conf. Am.* iv. 77 ff., *Heroid.* vii; *Conf. Am.* 147 ff., *Heroid.* i; *Conf. Am.* iv. 371 ff., *Met.* ix. 666 ff.; *Conf. Am.* iv. 451 ff., *Met.* ix. 666 ff.; *Conf. Am.* iv. 731 ff., *Heroid.* ii, *Remed. Am.* 591 ff.; *Conf. Am.* iv. 979 ff., *Met.* ii. 1 ff.; *Conf. Am.* iv. 1901 ff., *Heroid.* xiii; *Conf. Am.* iv. 2045 ff., *Met.* ix. 31 ff.; *Conf. Am.* iv. 2927 ff., *Met.* xi. 266 ff.; *Conf. Am.* iv. 3317 ff., *Met.* i. 588 ff.; *Conf. Am.* iv. 3515 ff., *Met.* xiv. 698 ff.

[2] *Conf. Am.* v. 141 ff., *Met.* xi. 85 ff.; *Conf. Am.* v. 635 ff., *Ars Am.* ii. 561 ff. The original source is Homer, *Od.* viii. 266 ff. *Conf. Am.* v. 3927 ff., *Met.* vii. 159 ff.; *Conf. Am.* v. 4573 ff., *Met.* iii. 356 ff.; *Conf. Am.* v. 5551 ff., *Met.* vi. 424 ff.; *Conf. Am.* v. 6145 ff., *Met.* ii. 569 ff.; *Conf. Am.* v. 6225 ff., *Met.* ii. 409 ff.; *Conf. Am.* v. 6713 ff., *Met.* iv. 192 ff.; *Conf. Am.* v. 6807 ff., *Fast.* ii. 305 ff.

In Book VI we read of the drunken quarrel which arose at the marriage of Pirithous.[1] Lastly, in Book VII, a story extracted from the rarely used *Tristia*, we read of the brazen bull constructed by the Sicilian tyrant Phalaris, in which human beings were roasted alive, whose first victim was its contriver, the enterprising scientific inventor of the period Perillus, whom by a blunder Gower calls Berillus ; and in conclusion we have the stories of Lycaon, and of the capture of Gabii by Arruns, son of the tyrant Tarquin.[2] Truly English literature through Gower owes a heavy debt to Ovid.

Chaucer and Gower gave vogue to Ovid, and his works were soon turned into English verse. Caxton translated the *Metamorphoses* as early as 1480 ; other versions followed, of which the most important are Turberville's *Heroides* (1567), Golding's *Metamorphoses* (1567), Underdown's *Ibis* (1569), Churchyard's *Tristia* (1580), the poet Marlowe's *Amores* (1597), and Browne's *Remedia Amoris* (1599). The earliest translation of the *Fasti* is that of John Gower (1640), a Cambridge graduate.

The sources of Spenser's glorious allegorical poem the *Faerie Queene* are complex, comprising Homer and Virgil, the old romances, Chaucer and the Italian poets. But Ovid too had his share in moulding Spenser's genius. The faculty of sustained narration and copious invention, the love of beauty,

---

[1] *Conf. Am.* vi. 485 ff., *Met.* xii. 210 ff.

[2] *Conf. Am.* vii. 3295 ff., *Trist.* iii. 11. 39 ff. The story is often alluded to by Ovid, *Ars Am.* i. 653, *Ibis* 437, *Trist.* v. 1. 53, *Pont.* ii. 9. 44, iii. 6. 42. *Conf. Am.* vii. 3355 ff., *Met.* i. 217 ff. ; *Conf. Am.* vii. 4593 ff., *Fast.* ii. 687 ff.

of the beauty of physical form, and the brightness
and grace of external nature, are features common
to these two poets.   Spenser found in Ovid a sympathetic nature, and gathered from him much of his
details.   Georgos, who was discovered by a ploughman in a furrow and brought up 'in ploughman's
state', is suggested by the similar upbringing of the
Etruscan Tages in Ovid (*F. Q.* i. 10. 66, *Met.* xv.
553).   Many of the legends of Ovid are briefly
retold by Spenser, or woven allusively into the rich
embroidery of the *Faerie Queene.*   The nymph that
was changed into a stone 'from which fresh streams
do flow' is Ovid's Arethusa (*F. Q.* ii. 2. 7 ff., *Met.*
v. 572 ff.).   Medea with 'her mighty charms, her
furious loving fit' (*F. Q.* ii. 12 44, *Met.* vii. 1 ff.),
' the fair Adonis turned to a flower' (*F. Q.* iii. 1. 34,
Met. x. 503 ff.), Narcissus 'Cephisus' foolish child',
Daphne, Hyacinthus, and 'fair Coronis' (*F. Q.* iii. 11.
36–7, *Met.* i. 452 ff., x. 162 ff., ii. 531 ff.), Phaethon,
who was ' bold to guide the chariot of the sun', the
'blindfold god' Cupid who shoots arrows 'some
headed with sad lead, some with pure gold', the gold
to cause love, the lead to dispel it (*F. Q.* iii. 11. 38,
Met. ii. 1 ff. ; *F. Q.* iii. 11. 48, *Met.* i. 469), Hippo·
lytus that ' of his own steeds was all to pieces torn ',
Hercules 'that strong Tirynthian swain ' (Ovid calls
him ' Tirynthius heros') that 'brought forth with
him' from the underworld Cerberus 'that dreadful dog
of Hell' (*F. Q.* v. 8. 43, *Met.* xv. 500 ; *F. Q.* vii. 12.
35, *Met.* vii. 410), are all cameos cut from the *Metamorphoses* and inset into the stately fabric of the
Faerie Queene.   Expressions of Ovid are borrowed

word for word, such as the realistic description of the
untimely end of the 'pagan hound', whom the knight
so utterly destroyed

> that no whole piece of him was to be seen
> > > (*F. Q.* v. 8. 42)

which is Ovid's

> > nullasque in corpore partes,
> Noscere quas posses ; unumque erat omnia vulnus

(*Met.* xv. 528).   These illustrations are from the
Metamorphoses, but Spenser borrows also from other
works of Ovid : thus 'the goodly golden fruit' with
which Acontius wooed Cydippe is from the *Heroides*
(*F. Q.* ii. 7. 55, *Heroid.* xx and xxi), and 'Arion
crowned', whose song charmed the dolphins, is from
the *Fasti* (*F. Q.* iv. 11. 23, *Fast.* ii. 105).

Shakespeare, the most romantic of dramatists, felt
the enchantment of Ovid's romance.   The 'small
Latin' that he knew certainly comprised some
knowledge of Ovid in the original Latin, acquired
no doubt at school, where Ovid formed part of the
ordinary curriculum.   In one or other of Shakespeare's
plays there are allusions to every one of the fifteen
books of the *Metamorphoses*.   Similarity of language
proves that Shakespeare frequently used Golding's
noble and melodious translation.   Prospero's address
(*Tempest*, v. 1. 33) :

Ye elves of hills, brooks, standing lakes and groves,
> > . . . by whose aid,
Weak masters though ye be, I have bedimm'd
The noontide sun, call'd forth the mutinous winds,
And 'twixt the green sea and the azured vault
Set roaring war : to the dread rattling thunder

Have I given fire ; . . . the strong based promontory
Have I made shake and by the spurs pluck'd up
The pine and cedar : graves at my command
Have waked their sleepers,

is suggested by Golding (vii. 265) :

Ye ayres and winds : ye elves of hills, of brooks, of
    woods alone,
Of standing lakes, and of the night approach ye
    everychone ;
Through help of whom . . .
By charms I make the calm seas rough, and make
    the rough seas playne,
And cover all the sky with clouds and chase them
    thence again ;
By charms I raise and lay the winds, . . .
Whole woods and forests I remove : I make the
    mountains shake,
And even the earth itself to groan and fearfully to
    quake ;
I call up dead men from their graves.

The description of the boar in *Venus and Adonis*
(619 ff.) :

On his bow-back he hath a battle set
Of bristly pikes, that ever threat his foes ;
His eyes like glowworms shine when he doth fret ; . . .
His brawny sides, with hairy bristles arm'd,
Are better proof than thy spear's point can enter,

closely follows Golding (*Met.* viii. 376) :

His eyes did glister blood and fire : right dreadful
    was to see
His brawned neck, right dreadful was his hair, which
    grew as thick
With pricking points as one of them could well by
    other stick.

And like a front of armed pikes set close in battle
ray
The sturdy bristles on his back stood staring up
alway.

But it is clear that Shakespeare was not indebted to
translations only for his knowledge of Ovid. In
Midsummer Night's Dream the name Titania is
taken directly from Ovid, who uses it as an epithet
of Diana (Phoebe), the sister of the sun-god Phoebus,
himself a Titan. In Golding the appellative Titania
is dropped, and Phoebe is used as the goddess's name ;
from which it is manifest that Shakespeare must have
got his Titania from the Latin original.[1] Minute
examination of *Venus and Adonis* reveals the same
result. Thus when Venus says of the boar (631) :

Alas ! he nought esteems that face of thine,

the word 'face' is clearly dictated by Ovid's 'non
movet aetas nec *facies*', not by Golding's 'thy
countenance fair and brave'.[2] But there is stronger
proof. In the *Rape of Lucrece* the story of Lucrece
and the iniquitous Tarquin is drawn from the concluding portion of Book II of Ovid's *Fasti*, and shows
in many passages an exact correspondence of language
and thought. Yet no translation of the *Fasti* into
English had at that time already been produced.

The statement of the acute contemporary critic

---

[1] Ovid, *Met.* iii. 173=Golding iii. 208. Ovid uses Titania also of
Latona (vi. 346), Pyrrha (i. 395), Circe (xiv. 382, 438). The name
Autolycus in *A Winter's Tale* appears to be taken from Ov.
Met. xi. 313.

[2] *Met.* x. 547=Golding x. 635. See Max Dürnhöfer, *Shakespeares
Venus und Adonis im Verhältniss zu Ovids Metamorphosen* (Halle,
1890), p. 35.

Francis Meres (1598) in *Palladis Tamia* is well known : 'As the soul of Euphorbus was thought to live in Pythagoras, so the sweet witty soul of Ovid lives in mellifluous and honey-tongued Shakespeare ; witness his *Venus and Adonis*, his *Lucrece*, his sugared sonnets among his private friends.' *Venus, and Adonis* is based on the *Metamorphoses* (x), *Lucrece* on the *Fasti* (ii). In the case of the *Sonnets* many of the ideas are drawn from the *Metamorphoses*. In Book XV of the *Metamorphoses* Ovid expounds in the mouth of the Greek philosopher Pythagoras his theory of the progress of the universe. Nature is in a state of constant rotation, 'all things are ever changing, nothing perishes' ('omnia mutantur, nihil interit,' *Met.* xv. 165). Time, the devourer, and old age consume all things (*ib.* 234), but only that they may return to their primary elements, from which they come back into life ; then the same order of existence is renewed once again (*id.* 249). Thus appearances of change are due to a constantly re-volving cycle. The same idea runs through Shake-speare's Sonnets, that 'there is nothing new, but that which is hath been before' (Sonnet lix), that 'Time that gave doth now his gift confound' (Sonnet lx), that there is 'nothing novel, nothing strange', but all things are 'but dressings of a former sight' (Sonnet cxxiii). The recurrence of natural phenomena is thus illustrated in Sonnet lx :

Like as the waves make towards the pebbled shore,
So do our minutes hasten to their end ;
Each changing place with that which goes before,
In sequent toil all forwards do contend.

This is borrowed from Ovid through Golding (Ov. *Met*. xv. 180 = Golding 201) : [1]

As every wave drives others forth, and that which
    comes behind
Both thrusteth and is thrust himself : even so the
    times by kind
Do fly and follow both at once, and evermore
    renew.

In Sonnet lxiv the reflexion,

> When I have seen the hungry ocean gain
> Advantage on the kingdom of the shore,
> And the firm soil win of the watery main,
> Increasing store with loss and loss with store ;
> When I have seen such interchange of state,

suggests the conclusion that ' Time will come, and take his love away '. The idea again is from Ovid through Golding (*Met*. xv. 262 = Golding 287) :

Even so have places oftentimes exchanged their
    estate,
And I have seen it sea which was substantial ground
    alate.[2]
Again where sea was, I have seen the same become
    dry land.

Analysis of the classical allusions in Shakespeare's plays proves that the influence of Ovid was at least five times as great as that of Virgil.[3] When the pedant Holofernes in *Love's Labour's Lost* (iv. 2. 127) remarks that ' for the elegancy, facility and golden cadence of poesy Ovidius Naso was the man '

---

[1] See *Quarterly Review*, No. 419, April 1900, pp. 455 foll., ' Ovid and Shakespeare's Sonnets,' by Sir Sidney Lee.

[2] alate = erected, raised up (*ala*, a wing).

[3] R. K. Root, *Classical Mythology in Shakespeare* (1903). p. 3.

—the man 'for smelling out the odoriferous flowers
of fancy, the jerks of invention', Shakespeare is no
doubt expressing his own opinion of his model poet.
Illustration is endless.

> Cupid's strongest bow ;
> and   'his best arrow with the golden head'

(*Midsummer Night's Dream*, i. 1. 169) is from Ovid
(*Met.* i. 469).   The tale of Pyramus and Thisbe in
Midsummer Night's Dream is from Ovid (*Met.* iv.
55 ff.).   When Jaques exclaims (*As You Like It*, iii.
3. 7), 'O knowledge, ill-inhabited, worse than Jove
in a thatched house,' he alludes to Ovid's description of the visit paid by Jupiter and Mercury to the
peasant couple Baucis and Philemon who lived in
a cottage 'coped with thatch' (Golding, *Met.* viii.
626 ff.).   The long list of flowers let fall by Proserpina
when she was carried off by Dis (*Winter's Tale*, iv.
4. 116) is from Ovid (*Met.* v. 389 ff.).

> Ariadne passioning
> For Theseus' perjury and unjust flight

is from Ovid (*Heroid.* x).   The sentiment in *Romeo
and Juliet*,

> At lovers' perjuries, they say, Jove laughs,

is translated from Ovid (*Ars Am.* i. 633),

> Iuppiter ex alto periuria ridet amantum.

Even the doleful *Tristia*, which lamentations were
composed by ' the most capricious poet, honest Ovid,
among the Goths' (*As You Like It*, iii. 3. 9 ; cp.
Trist. iii. 12. 55), supplies Shakespeare with an
illustration (*2 Henry VI*, v. 2. 57) :

Meet I an infant of the house of York,
Into as many gobbets will I cut it,
As wild Medea young Absyrtus did.

Ovid tells in the *Tristia* (iii. 9. 6) how Medea killed
and cut up her brother Absyrtus, and scattered his
limbs in order that her father Aeetes might be
stopped in his pursuit of her while collecting them.

With Ben Jonson it is different. Although the
mind and memory of that great dramatist were
saturated with classical learning, Jonson's works
reveal little impress of the influence of Ovid. There
is one notable exception. In the curious and complex satirical drama *The Poetaster* a by-plot is inserted
into the main action of the play regarding a supposed
intrigue of the poet Ovid with the princess Julia, the
emperor's daughter, culminating in a profane banquet
of the gods, in which Ovid, Julia, and others travesty
the characters of the divinities. This banquet, which
is based on an account of such a blasphemous orgy
in which Augustus himself took part according to
Suetonius (*Aug.* 70), is interrupted by the unexpected
arrival of the incensed emperor, who banishes Ovid
from court and imprisons Julia (Act iv, sc. 3). At
the beginning of the play Ovid, as a young man, is
introduced, repeating selections from his poems,
which are rendered by Jonson into English verse
(Act i, sc. 1). Then Ovid's father appears, and in
the character of the prudent parent expresses dis-
approval of poetry as a pursuit for his son, and counsels
him to abandon it in favour of the more practical
profession of the law. The great Homer, 'the god
of poets,' whose immortality the young Ovid hopes to

rival, 'what was he ? a poor blind rhyming rascal that
scarce ever made a good meal in his sleep, the hungry
beggar.'   Later Ovid explains to his friend Tibullus
that he writes his very law exercises in verses, 'they
run from my pen unwittingly, if they be verse.'   In
these passages, as in others, Jonson follows Ovid's
words so closely as almost to translate them.[1] But the
result is stilted, and the impression gathered is that
Jonson had little real appreciation of the excellences
of Ovid.

The lesser lights among the Elizabethans also
turned to Ovid.   Drayton's *England's Heroical
Epistles* (1597) are modelled on the *Heroides*.   Chap-
man's affected *Ovid's Banquet of Sense* (1595) is
inspired by the *Amores* and *Tristia*.   Heywood's
prolix and tedious classical plays ' *The Golden, The
Silver, The Brazen*, and *The Iron Age*' (1611–1632)
are a patchwork of stories selected from the
Metamorphoses, that of Callisto, Absyrtus, the death
of Hercules, the Calydonian boar hunt, and so forth.
His *Rape of Lucrece* and *Apollo and Daphne* are
from the same source.   Shirley's *Contention of Ajax
and Ulysses* (1659), chiefly known through the
splendid song in the last scene,

> The glories of our blood and state
> Are shadows, not substantial things,

is a spirited adaptation of the famous debate at the
beginning of the thirteenth book of the *Metamor-*

---

[1] Act i, sc. 1.   Ov. *Trist.* iv. 10. 21 ff.:

> Saepe pater dixit ' studium quid inutile temptas ?
> Maeonides nuilas ipse reliquit opes . . .'
> Sponte sua carmen numeros veniebat ad aptos,
> Et quod temptabam dicere versus erat.

phoses, in which the two heroes assert their respective claims to inherit the arms of Achilles. Shirley follows Ovid's language very closely, and translates him though with a considerable amount of expansion. Similar expansion appears in the same poet's *Narcissus, the self-lover*, in which Ovid's story of Narcissus and the nymph Echo (*Met.* iii. 339 ff.) is retold at great length. Interest in Ovid's personality produced the curious Restoration drama of Sir Aston Cokain, *The Tragedy of Ovid*, which treats of the poet's exile, and is based on the *Tristia* and *Epistulae ex Ponto*.

After the Restoration came a race of writers in little sympathy with the romantic movement. Their greatest is Dryden, one of the foremost English men of letters, the most effective master of satire since the Roman Juvenal. Satire makes men ill-tempered and analytic. But when he was old and broken Dryden's sunny nature turned from criticism to romance. Conscious of his own supreme skill in narration he published in 1700, the year of his death, the *Fables*, translated or adapted from Homer Chaucer and Boccaccio, but far the greatest number of them from Ovid. The selection made by Dryden is important as showing which stories were best in the judgement of this excellent critic. He chose to transfuse into his vigorous verse the legends of Meleager and Atalanta, Baucis and Philemon, Pygmalion and the statue, Cinyras and Myrrha, Ceyx and Alcyone ; and he translated also the entire Twelfth and most of the Thirteenth and Fifteenth Books of the *Metamorphoses*.

On modern English poetry Ovid's influence is less extensive. The glittering mine has yielded its ore to many workers, and poets have sought other quarries. Also the subjective and introspective attitude of modern poetry is antipathetic to the Roman mode. Still the masterful force of Ovid has from time to time asserted itself, and his plentiful materials have supplied fresh themes of beauty for creative genius. His story of ' earth's white daughter' Arethusa has been retold by Shelley with musical energy which surpasses the original in splendour : his legend of Perseus and Andromeda has reappeared in the rushing torrent of Kingsley's hexameters.[1] The song of Callicles in Matthew Arnold's *Empedocles on Etna*,

> And there, they say, two bright and aged snakes,
> Who once were Cadmus and Harmonia,
> Bask in the glens or on the warm sea-shore,

is a resetting of a portion of the *Metamorphoses*.[2] The substance of Swinburne's *Atalanta in Calydon* is derived mainly from Ovid's full and spirited narrative : William Morris has not disdained to borrow from Ovid the story of Pygmalion and the Image told in the *Earthly Paradise* : Austin Dobson has reproduced in delicate verse Ovid's tragic tale of the death of Procris ' among the white wind-flowers shot

---

[1] Ov. *Met.* v. 572 ff., iv. 706 ff.

[2] *Empedocles on Etna*, Act i, sc. 2. Ov. *Met.* iv. 562 ff. The original Greek source was Euripides' *Bacchae*, 1330 ff., and a lost play of Euripides, see frag. 922. Cp. Milton, *P. L.* ix. 505, ' never since of serpent-kind Lovelier, not those that in Illyria changed Hermione (*sic*) and Cadmus.'

in the throat' inadvertently by her hunter husband Cephalus.[1]

It was a sorry act of blind despotism that dispatched Ovid to die in exile on the frosty shore of the Euxine, it was the senseless act of a moral pedant who knew no mercy. But though Augustus could rid Rome of its greatest poet, he could not silence that poet's voice, which death cannot touch. Ovid knew his own immortality, and has asserted it in two elegiac couplets, which are among the finest in all the stately Roman language (*Trist.* iv. 9. 21):

> Ibit ad occasum quicquid dicemus ab ortu,
>   Testis et Hesperiae vocis Eous erit.
> Trans ego tellurem, trans altas audiar undas,
>   Et gemitus vox est magna futura mei.

> From sun to sun the words I write shall reach,
> The East shall witness to my Western speech.
> Across the billowy deep and every clime
> My voice shall echo till the end of time.

[1] *Met.* viii. 260 ff., *Met.* x. 243 ff. Austin Dobson, *Collected Poems*, p. 167. *Met.* vii. 661 ff.

SATURA AND SATIRE

By R. J. E. TIDDY

THE name which has been chosen for this lecture may, I am afraid, savour of pedantry. But there is a reason for the choice. *Satura* means something very different from Satire. They have often been confused; it was very natural that English satirists of the sixteenth and seventeenth centuries, for instance, should shut their eyes to the distinction, and it is on the whole well that they did. They gave their attention to a very entertaining form of literature, and they adorned it. But they leave us one regret: they neglected a native form akin to satire, but different, and far more closely akin to *Satura*, a form in which they might have done brilliant things. For the happiest work of the English satirists is in those non-satirical digressions which they allow themselves from the more exciting business of lashing ' the Town ' and castigating vice.

> An humble cot entapissed with mosse,
> A lowlie life that fears no sodaine losse,
> A mind that dreads no fall, that craves no crowne,
> But makes his true content his best renowne,
> These are the choice contents, the goods, the gaine
> Which rightly can be ours——the rest are vaine.

These sentiments of Lodge,[1] worth a great deal of invective, have an ancestry reaching perhaps to the very beginnings of Latin literature. They are a survival in Satire from that earlier form of ethical writing which was *Satura*. But in spite of their Roman ancestry they have a curiously English tone. They touch, in fact, on an ideal common to the two peoples. The strange thing is that they are on the whole so rare in English satire; but the reason is to be sought in the history of pre-Renaissance satire in England, and in the development of satire at Rome.

But consider first the extent of classical influence in English satire. It is more imperious and overmastering than in any other form. Narrative poetry suffered much from the domination of the classical epic—'the greatest work of human nature,' as it seemed to the seventeenth century. But from that iron discipline emerged some of the virtue of *Paradise Lost* as well as the frigid self-complacency of Blackmore's *Prince Arthur*. If one may still speak of periods in English literature (I think one may with as much truth as we have a right to expect in anything), there are periods when the native genius can absorb unharmed almost any quantity of foreign matter, others when it sickens and dies. And except in such periods as these latter, except we may say in the late seventeenth and the early eighteenth centuries, the national spirit in narrative, in drama, and in lyric has shown a splendid immunity; whether in resisting or in admitting the classical infection, it has been renewed and strengthened. But in England

---

[1] *A Fig for Momus*, Satyre 5.

native satire succumbed with hardly a struggle to classical influence, became in fact classical as hardly any other kind of literature did. The reason is obvious. A very small part, and by no means the highest, of the poet's nature can be devoted to the condemnation of his fellow men. The plain man reserves it for his after-dinner hours of ease, as a well-understood convention of amusement. To make a business of it is the act of the fanatic or the journalist, and the journalist is far commoner than the fanatic. So satire is the prey of fashion, because it has no heart. Waller writes an 'Advice to a Painter'; Denham turns it to satiric purposes, and for seven years that fashion reigns. Rochester suggests an adaptation of Juvenal, and that fashion reigns for a century. It was precisely the same when Lodge and Donne opened their satires with a line or two from Horace, and 'under fained private names noted generall vices'. Satire has thus always been a favourite field for the literary historian and for the tracing of influences and developments, but the great critics have given it little attention.

Now if you look at the history of satire in England, you will find that the pure form of it, the negative criticism which insists wholly on the frailty of our mortal nature, has never been very characteristic of our temperament. We are, it is agreed, most prone to humour and to genial tolerance, and when Shakespeare writes *Troilus and Cressida*, we rack our brains for an explanation. It is true that fairly typical Englishmen of supreme talents, like Pope, and at least one man of genius, Swift, chose the

satiric form for some of their best work.   But they
fall well within the only markedly critical era of our
literature.   From time to time a disappointed man
of the world will steal away, as Wyatt did from Court,
and take the only consolation left him in the condemnation of mankind.   But we have never quite
achieved an English Juvenal.   And if you turn to
the origins, there is no Old English satire.   In
Beowulf there is nothing nearer to it than the speech
of Unferth, the single idealized echo which has
survived of the quarrels that must often have
divided the warriors flushed with the gold-giver's
ale.   Flyting was a conventional development of
such quarrels ; but this was far more popular in
Scotland than in the South.   England did indeed
give at least its share to the large body of mediaeval
Latin satire on the scandals of the Church, written
as a rule by the clerks in minor orders who were
themselves perhaps the Church's gravest scandal.
And this satire has much in common with Classical
Latin satire.   Its spirit is almost wholly negative.
It is an art product.   Like most Roman satire, it
carries with it little conviction of moral earnestness,
but aims at wit, and attains it,—a quainter, more
' Gothic' wit than the Roman, but in many ways, for
instance in its skilful adaptation and parody, very
near to the Latin models.   It parodies the Vulgate
as Juvenal uses Vergil and Statius, and tags its
verses with lines of Juvenal just as Juvenal himself
quotes Lucilius.   One stanza seems to exhibit most
of the qualities of this literature :

Diligit episcopus hilarem datorem,
Fas et nefas ausus post muneris odorem,
Nescius resumere post lapsum pudorem
Eiectum semel attrita de fronte ruborem.[1]

Here is the pessimism of Juvenal, in Juvenal's very
words.   But for all that, this Goliardic satire is not
English, it belongs to the cosmopolitan culture of the
Church.   One cannot after all quite ignore the fact
that it is written in Latin.   Anglicized it assumes
the spirit of the Prologue to *The Canterbury Tales*,
or of the gay victim of the 'erchedeknes' court,
whose impenitent but unquotable lyric is printed in
Wright's *Political Songs*.[2]

The native literature which, before 1595, roughly
fills the place of classical satire centres, as may be
expected, around religion and politics.   There are
sermons, and ballads of poor folk in revolt, there are
also the diatribes of ecclesiastical or political controversy, there are the vehement personal quarrels
of Skelton and the amenities of Martin Marprelate.
None of these is exactly satire.   Most of them are
written under the smart of an urgent grievance and
have as a rule only a temporary value.   So that the
Political Songs are more interesting to history than
to literature; their authors did not rise much above
the level of the pamphleteer or the lampoonist.
The Sermon is obviously beyond my scope.   One
does not look to it either for the satirist's despair of

---

[1] Wright, *Political Songs*, Camden Society's Publications, 1839,
p. 32.   'The bishop loveth a cheerful giver : on the scent of a 'present'
he will dare right or wrong ; and once he has lost his sense of shame,
he can never get back a blush to his brazen face.'

[2] p. 155.

human destiny, or for the alternative of genial tolerance. As I hope to show, the body of native satiric literature, where it assumes a more general aim, indeed often in unexpected places, assumes also the temperate and kindly qualities of our race. But in the main it is purely negative. And therefore Latin satire, bearing majestically down upon it with its wider outlook on society, with an elaborate art underlying its assumed nonchalance of form, and with all its apparatus of rhetoric and epigram, made short work of the artless native product. For the lampoon and the ballad and the abusive pamphlet, it substituted a form of literature which, whatever its limitations, could have a permanent application, and could express not merely the grievance of the moment, but the whole critical temperament and outlook on life.

Satire in this sense, like the 'Character' and the Essay, came into being when society became urban and self-conscious. Men began to study the curiosities of their kind, and therefore their frailties. Questioning everything, yet still burdened by a heavy weight of authority, by imperious sovereigns and vigilant archbishops, they took sides acrimoniously but were forced to mask their discord under the pretence of generalities. In Latin satire, thrown open to them like the rest of classical literature by the same impulse of scientific study, they found the 'fained names of certain Romaine ' ready to their hands. The wider outlook was at first illusory; the earliest 'classical' satirists in English are lampoonists ill-disguised. But one good

gift classical satire brought at once, form. It taught
the satirist how to begin and how to end, and in
satire at least that is half of the whole.

Yet these gains brought corresponding losses.
The political satire of so early a date as the thirteenth
and fourteenth centuries had sometimes a touch of
the charm of the traditional songs—a delightful
refrain for instance, as in the Ballad on the defeat
of Richard, Earl of Cornwall, at Lewes :

> Richard, though thou be ever trichard,
> Trichen shalt thou never more.[1]

Or you will find a song of the sorrows of the
oppressed husbandman put into the husbandman's
mouth, with some of the satirist's rage, but with an
insight and a pathos which speak of the folk-poet
rather than the satirist.[2] Again among these songs
on the evils of the times there comes, with a frequency
hard to parallel in classical satire, a desire to mend
matters and a hope of better things. These positive
touches help to convince us of the sincerity even of
the most frightful denunciations of human wickedness.
They secure, for instance, for the author of *Piers
Plowman* a warm place in affections which might
otherwise be a little alienated by the sustained can-
dour of Lady Meed and the Seven Deadly Sins.
Piers Plowman indeed shows the possibilities and
the limitations of native English satire most strikingly.
Formless, discursive, full of lively pictures and racy
talk, it ranges over the whole of society and signally
fails to comprehend it in a general grasp. And it

---

[1] Wright, *Political Songs*, p. 69.   [2] Ibid., p. 149.

has this great merit, that in its most passionate condemnation of sin it reveals neither a perfect hatred
nor a complete despair of sinners. It may be
objected that this is just not the merit of satire.
And this certainly is not the satire of the Elizabethans, nor of Oldham and Dryden, nor of Pope
and Churchill. But, curiously enough, in this respect
Piers Plowman and the works of its kind do closely
resemble *Satura*.

The history of satire in the modern sense of the
word begins at Rome with Lucilius. But before him
can be dimly seen, and after him more clearly, a kind
of writing, that of Varro, of Horace sometimes, of
Petronius and Seneca, which, though it had affinities
with Lucilian satire, was yet a very different thing.
And this was *Satura*. It was not by any means
wholly a native product. Quintilian's famous claim,
that *Satura* was wholly Roman, has rather less truth
than most of those sweeping statements by which
literary criticism seeks to arrest the attention of
a yawning world. The first known writer of *Satura*
was Ennius, an extraordinarily versatile artist, born
in 239 B.C. in a bilingual Italian town where Oscan
and Greek and probably very little Latin were
spoken. It seems likely that he first learnt Latin
perfectly in the army. He was an honoured depen-
dant of the aristocratic hellenizing class, as were
most of the pioneers of Latin literature. In all his
other work he tried with wonderful success to adapt
Greek forms, Greek metre and mythology, to the
Latin language, and in *Satura* it seems that he did
the same.

Unfortunately we have no trustworthy evidence at all for any native germs of *Satura* which Ennius may have found, and only grotesquely meagre fragments of his own work in this kind.   In the face of these circumstances it may be held that no comment is so becoming as a respectful silence.   But the obvious division of Roman satire into two streams does stimulate inquiry ; and, further, the fragments of Ennius do suggest that he belonged to the warmer stream of the two, that he admitted other things into his satire besides what Dryden called ' the defamation of others '.

It is agreed that the word *Satura* means a medley, a miscellany.   It may be derived from the religious ritual, from the offering of the full plate of mixed bakemeats, or it may be a metaphor from the kitchen, meaning a ' stuffing ', or, as Juvenal apparently thought, an *olla podrida*.   At any rate, the phrase *per saturam* (' in a stew,' ' mixed up together ') was transferred to other activities, and Ennius could call some of his poems *saturae*.   Now these are in different metres.   Is that then all that *Satura* means, a collection of poems in different metres ?   This is the trend of modern belief about it.   Myself, I believe it is wrong.   The title meant that the contents of the whole collection were miscellaneous, the metres various, and probably even that some of the single poems were discursive. What is not implied in the title was nevertheless from the first an element of *Satura*, some sort of dramatic quality.   Such a form exactly suits all that we know of the original Latin temperament.   The

primitive Romans' most natural form of expression
would be, in their more serious mood, a practical
comment on life in general, with a strong utilitarian
bias; in their lighter mood, the character-sketch in
dramatic form, verging on caricature. The discur-
siveness of *Satura* and its lack of unity would sit
naturally on a people whose native sense of form in
art was even slighter than our own. Some few
fragments have survived, no doubt in a distorted
form, of a *Carmen de Moribus* (a *Moral Ode*),
ascribed to the elder Cato, whose life is even now
almost proverbial for its quaint conservatism. The
fragments show something very like the serious side
of *Satura*. ''Twas our fathers' way to dress seemly
abroad, in the house sufficiently. They paid more
for their horses than for their cooks.' ' The life of
man is like iron ; use it and it wears out : if you
don't use it, still the rust destroys it. So we see men
are worn out by work : if you do no work, sloth and
idleness do you more harm than work.'[1] If Cato
wrote this, it is the contribution of one who would
have no truck with poetry; but it shows nevertheless
what sort of sentiments would have found their way
into earlier Roman verse.[2] The holiday mood of
primitive Rome still survives in some measure
among the plays of Plautus, though thickly overlaid
with Hellenism. But one need go no farther than
the popular theatres of modern Italian towns to find
most of the livelier features of *Satura*.

Of these native origins of *Satura* you can find

---

[1] Baehrens, *Fragmenta Poetarum Romanorum*, p. 57.
[2] Cf. also the *Praecepta* and *Sententiae*.

traces in Ennius.   ' I never write verse unless I have
the gout.'   ' It does one a world of harm, i' faith, to
dine too well.'   ' He ' (or perhaps ' she ') ' isn't always
asking for hot mustard and the tearful onion '[1]—
moral maxim and character-sketch are both there.
Here again, perhaps, is an echo of the witticisms of
the village holiday :

> Nam qui lepide postulat alterum frustrari
> Quem frustratur frustra eum dicit frustrasse ;
> Nam qui se frustrari quem frustra sentit,
> Frustratur, si frustra est ; ille non est frustra.[2]

All this is rude and of the soil, but at least it does
not err on the side of severity.   The early *Satura*
was mild ; and it was also hospitable.   It accepted
Greek subject-matter from the first.   Ennius drew
on Aesop's fables, described a debate between Life
and Death which seems to be derived from Greek,
and possibly included in *Satura* a Roman version of
the ἐγκώμιον, a eulogy of his patron Scipio.   This
last has four lines at least of poetry of the high
Roman fashion :

> Longe Mundus caeli vastus constitit silentio,
> Et Neptunus saevus undis asperis pausam dedit ;
> Sol equis iter repressit ungulis volantibus,
> Constitere amnes perennes, arbores vento vacant.[3]

---

[1] Baehrens, *op. cit.*, Ennius, 488, 456, 477.

[2] Ibid. 479.   Untranslatable.   It may be paraphrased : The man who
thinks to score a pretty score off another, says that he has scored off
him off whom he would score,—but he hasn't, all the same.   For he
who thinks he 's scoring, but isn't all the same, if he *isn't* all the same,
is scored off himself—and so the other scores.

[3] Baehrens, *op. cit.*, Ennius, 467. 'Then the great world of the heaven

The qualities likely to have been found in the earliest
familiar Latin literature are all to be seen in the
Satura of Ennius—prudential maxims not too
seriously pressed, simple jokes, and a free range of
subject which perhaps includes the possibility of
elevated descriptive verse.   But of satire in the
accepted sense there is not a trace.

Lucilius, Varro, Horace, in a less degree Juvenal,
all derive some features from their homely parentage.
All show some tendency to dramatic form, at any
rate all break freely and easily into dialogue.   The
setting of their satire is always the familiar life of
every day.   Most of them, for instance, describe
a dinner-party; Lucilius and Horace a journey;
Lucilius, Varro and Horace, a dialogue between
master and slave.   They all observe constantly a
close personal relationship with their readers, Juvenal
indeed least of all, and theirs is the easy language
of personal gossip with friends.   But only one of
them, Varro, keeps much of the savour of the country
market-day and the talk of farmers.   It is plainly
visible under a veneer of Greek fable and even of
Greek vocabulary.   Varro is surprisingly like those
figures of the early English Renaissance, Latimer,
Elyot, Ascham, who blended with the perilous
delights of the new learning a temperate puritanism,
and the sound morality which they saw, or thought
they saw, in the national past.   Precisely in the
spirit of these pioneers Varro emphasized in Greek

stood fast in silence, and the fierce Sea-god lulled awhile his raging
waves, and the Sun stayed the beating of his horses' flying hooves, and
the trees had respite from the winds.'

ethics what he thought he found in it of old Roman virtue. He praises the housekeeping of old Rome, as Ascham the archery of old England. 'So in the old days religion was held sacred and everything was holy.'[1] 'The wife would spin her wool and keep her eye on the porridge-pot to see it didn't burn.' 'The visitor had the pantry, the locks and keys, the meat-racks, the wine-casks, at his disposal, ... had the food in front of him, and sat well-fed at another's cost, without a thought for what's gone or what's to come, but with just one eye turned towards the kitchen door.'[2] There is a vein of satiric humour in this. It has not the naïve earnestness of Ascham, but if it smiles at this manifestation, it is full of sympathetic admiration for the moral spirit, for the generosity of the past. There is also plenty in Varro of the other side of the picture, satire of the follies of the present; for instance, a most racy enumeration of a lady's charms, which has been supposed to be a burlesque of the hellenized Roman's description of his mistress. 'In front of her ears from her tiny knot of hair hung six tiny twisted curls, and the tiny black pupils of her little twinkling eyes, what a merry little soul they showed!'[3] Varro's scourge is light! Marston has a picture of the courtier lover which, if one may judge by Varro's isolated fragment, illustrates well the difference between Varronian satire and the other type which impressed itself on the Elizabethans.

---

[1] Merry, *Fragments of Roman Poetry*, p. 206.
[2] Ibid., p. 209 sq.   [3] Ibid., p. 216.

His chamber hang'd about with elegies,
With sad complaints of his loves miseries;
His windows strew'd with sonnets, and the glasse
Drawne full of love-knots.   I approacht the asse,
And straight he weepes, and sighs some sonnet out
To his faire love!   And then he goes about
For to perfume her rare perfection
With some sweet-smelling pinck epitheton;
Then with a melting looke he writhes his head,
And straight in passion riseth in his bed;
And having kist his hand, stroke up his haire,
Made a French conge, cryes ' O cruel faire '
To the antique bed-post.[1]

Varro's humorous sympathy was native to him
and perhaps native to *Satura*.   But even in this
Greek influence can be traced.   According to Cicero
he followed Menippus of Gadara, and Menippus no
doubt helped to keep Varro's satire sweet upon his
tongue.   In one of Lucian's dialogues Diogenes the
Cynic sends a message from the world below by
Pollux to Menippus.   'You will know him when
you see a bald old man, with a coat " full of doors ",
open to every wind that blows, and embroidered with
a lot of patches.   And he is *always laughing*, and
jesting as a rule at quack philosophers.' [2]   This was
the sunny way of Greek satire, and it was wholesome
for Roman *Satura*.   The passage just quoted shows
that Varro may have followed Menippus when he
developed the homely moral maxim of agricultural
Rome into more formal discussions of philosophic
systems.   This change was inevitable when Latin

---

[1] Satyre III.
[2] *Dialogues of the Dead*, I. § 2.

thought became hellenized, and all Varro's successors in one way or another touch on philosophy.
In time the philosopher becomes one of the con-
ventions of *Satura*, like the travelled adventurer or
the 'changeling motley humourist' of Elizabethan
satire.

Though Varro is not the most typical of the Latin
satirists, the loss of so much of his work is a very great
misfortune. For besides his most strictly literary
gifts he has the sound sense to try to make his
generation better in the only effective way, not by
trouncing them, but by talking to them quietly.
The elements of satire as it left his hands are
remarkably like the several features of the teeming
mass of Elizabethan familiar literature. He might
have suggested an English 'miscellany' where Overbury's Dairymaid and Earle's Shee-precise Hypocrite
could have found a common home, to which the
Broadside Ballad, the Essay, the Song-book, and even
the Novel, might each have contributed something.
But the Elizabethans knew not Varro, but Casaubon's
mention of him, and the Essay and the Novel passed
on untouched. There is nothing here for regret,
except that when at last an example of English
Satura after the manner of Varro does appear, it is
so good. I mean *The Task*. Its likeness to Varro's
Satura is of course an accidental, not a family likeness.
Yet Cowper's *Task* bears out what I said of the
parallel between native English and early Roman
satire. For it reverts, partly through its Puritan
ancestry, but chiefly of course through the character
of its author, to the spirit of the pre-Renaissance

English satire. Though it is darkened a little by
the gloom and peevishness of religious mania, and
tinged a little still by the classical tradition of invective, that is not enough to exclude from it kindly
humour and sympathy and pathos, rare in English
satire after the classical influence had begun.

From about 130–100 B.C., beginning, that is to say,
at least thirty or forty years before Varro, Lucilius,
drawing, like Varro, upon Greek literature, had
originated a very different strain of *Satura*. He had
turned chiefly to the Old Comedy of Athens, the
most freely abusive literature perhaps that he knew.[1]
Lucilius was a man of different social position from
Ennius, and in temperament the exact antithesis
of Varro. When Gascoigne in his curiously old-
fashioned satire, *The Steele Glass*, appeals to the
authority of Lucilius, 'that worthy man,' and Hall, the
future bishop, hopes for some 'raging rough Lucile'
to spring from 'the ashes of his quiet style', neither
of them quite knew for what he was asking. Lucilius
was not strictly a worthy man. He was a man of
property, but he was always in debt; a member of the
cultured Scipionic circle, but a man of pleasure, cham-
pioning the bachelor's life against the attacks of the
sort of people who advocated large families. He is
the first satirist in the Elizabethan sense mainly
because he is the first writer of *Satura* who was also
a political partisan. Sometimes he consented to be
the literary weapon of the mildly democratic Scipios
in their family and political quarrel with the Metelli.

---

[1] It seems likely also that he drew on Latin folk-poetry, especially
on the Fescennine verse.

Sometimes as a provincial, but always as a gentleman
and a soldier, he prosecuted his private controversies
with Lupus, or Mucius the praetor.   There is not
a vestige of genuine moral indignation in him.   But
he was an unrivalled master of an abusive and obscene
vocabulary, and wore naturally the bluff manners of
the soldier on a nature cultivated but never refined.
It was in this way that he stamped *Satura* for ever
with the character of invective, profoundly influenced
Horace, and through him Persius, was the avowed
master of Juvenal, and through these an influence on
all later formal satire.   But not all even of Lucilius
is satire.   He wrote quite often in the purely familiar
and epistolary style ; the account, for instance, of his
journey to Sicily, where his chief cowman, Symmachus,
lay at death's door with lung trouble.   He chats cheer-
fully of the state of the roads.   ' Here it was all
child's play, just uphill and downhill everywhere, up
and down we went and it was all child's play and fun.
But when we came to the Setine country, then the
hard work began, sheer mountains, Etnas all and
jagged Athoses.' [1]   The Setine hills were of course
quite gentle slopes.   He writes of the scarcity of
oysters at one inn, of the curiously unattractive diet
of the provincials—boiled rue-stems in bowls to which
clung the remains of the boiled rue-stems of earlier
meals.   He scatters among his satire epitaphs of his
slaves and literary and grammatical criticism, the
criticism judicial rather than sympathetic, as becomes the satirist, but not severe.   It comes to
this, that Lucilius did not attempt to get rid of all

[1] ll. 110 sqq.

the geniality or all the pleasant rambling vein of older *Satura*.

The two main currents of Roman *Satura* were started on their course by Lucilius and Varro, and their successors added nothing of moment to the stream. I may therefore now briefly consider English classicising satire, and, as the history of its development requires it, point out the qualities of the Roman models.

The English adaptations of classical satire, if we except the isolated experiment of Wyatt, begin with a translation, the *Medicinable Morall of* Thos. Drant, *that is, the two Bookes of Horace his Satyres, Englyshed according to the prescription of Saint Hierome* (1566). Considerable traces survive in Drant of the older English satire. His aim is honest and sincere, to discover hypocrites; for 'the godly oft-tymes are not so much had in pryce as their counterfaits, dissembling naughty packs'. And so he deals freely with Horace. ' I have done as the people of God were commanded to do with their women that were hansome and beautiful. I have shaved off his (Horace's) hair and pared off his nails—that is I have wiped away all his vanity and superfluity of matter.' Thus the five lines in which Horace bids us go to the ant [1] appear in this form :

Not much unlyke the lytle ant (a beast of tydye toil)
Who drawes and dragges her delycates orewharte
    the hillie soyle
By myghte of mouth, in all she may, and placed in her
    cell,

---

[1] *Sat.* I. 1. 33 sqq.

She stickleth and bestirres herself, she huswyfes it
    right well.
She carves it fyne and mings it thicke and shrowdes
    it under roofe,
As one that of the wynter's wrath were not to learn
    the proofe,
Ne yet to care for after clappes, whereby when
    Janyuere,
That myrethe all the costs with slete, and saddes the
    'ginning year,
With aspere showrs doth cause the clouds and welken
    aye to wepe,
Then Lady Pismyer stirrs nowhere, she's clasped in
    closet deepe,
She keeps her Chrystenmasse in cave, and there they
    make bone cheare . . .

Contrast all this with the behaviour of man! This
ready and easy way with the classics was valuable not,
of course, because it wiped away their vanity, but
because it left room for the play of sympathy and
humour, more positive elements than satire was hereafter to show. Drant's example was naturally ignored.
But where you would least expect it, in Nash's *Four
Letters Confuted*,[1] there is a lively protest against the
unbroken gloom of mere satire—against Horace's,
Persius's and Juvenal's 'unsugred pills, however
excellently medicinable, yet harsh in the swallowing'.
The protest is welcome, though it is of course unfair
to Horace. But nothing came of it. For after
Casaubon's lectures at Geneva and Montpellier in
praise of Persius, the Elizabethan satirists decided
to echo the words of Horace and Juvenal, whom they
read, but to copy the manner, still more severe as

[1] R. B. McKerrow, vol. I, p. 284.

they supposed, of Persius, whom most of them did
not read. The manner but not the matter. For
Persius has just the quality which they lacked. He
is the only one of the three great Roman satirists who
was sincere in an avowed determination to reform
mankind. For all his boyish ambition to put things
cleverly and obscurely he was a good young man
with a noble purpose. The traditional life of him
tells us that he was of the most amiable character, of
a maidenly modesty, handsome, and distinguished by
the most dutiful affection for his mother, his sister, and
his aunt. This is high praise. But the evidence of
his satire indirectly bears out this testimony. He ear-
nestly wanted to make the idle young debauchee and
Philistine of Nero's Rome get up early, live cleanly,
and work. And with the idealism of youth, the in-
ducement he offers them is the Stoic philosophy.
His high creed is summed up in the two famous lines
which he has bequeathed to posterity—' Virtutem
videant intabescantque relicta '[1] and the untranslatable ' Tecum habita : noris quam sit tibi curta
supellex '.[2] Stoicism by the very completeness of its
abnegation wins some of the beauty of more positive
creeds, and it is no wonder that the puritan Casaubon
preferred Persius to the other two. But the force
of his preference did not very profoundly affect the
Elizabethan satirists. A few passages of Hall are
inspired by him, but the others remembered only that
Persius wrote a prologue and had a crabbed style.

---

[1] ' Let them look on lost virtue and pine at her loss.'

[2] Literally ' Live with yourself' (i. e. at home alone) ' and learn how
scanty is your furniture '. (iv. 52.)

To them he was pre-eminently one of those Roman ancients

Whose words were short and darksome was their sense,
Who reads one line of their harsh poesies
Thrice must he take his wind, and breath him thrice.

Horace was naturally more to the taste of the Elizabethans, as of all succeeding satirists. But he appeals perhaps even more strongly to those who are not satirists. Here at last is an artist, and one who, alone of the Roman satirists of whom much survives, makes *Satura* a means of *complete* self-expression. He tells the truth, no doubt, when he says that he had to suffer envy and defamation, but it never soured him. His very defence is a model of restraint, in which he tells no more than the plain truth. He had no enthusiasms and no principles, unless reverence for good taste and common sense can be called a principle. For his satires at once expound and manifest the rule of tact. Though an avowed follower of Lucilius, simply by temperament he reverts to the style of Varro. He is hardly a satirist at all, still less is he a moralist. 'Folly is his proper quarry,' said Dryden, and we may add to folly bad manners. Yet once or twice, half playfully, he lets us see his principle at work. 'This'—he speaks of his father's teaching, the freedman father at whom his rivals sneered—'This saved me from the vices which ruin a man, left me with mild and venial faults. Perhaps they will be lessened by the lapse of time, a friend's free speech, my own reflection. For in my study or on my walks I do my duty by

myself. "Yes," I say; "that is the right course";
or "If I do this I shall live a better life"; or "This is
the way to be welcome to one's friends"; or "That
was not pleasant in So-and-so; shan't I perhaps
some day do something unawares as bad as he?"[1]
In such words Horace reveals the rule of tact not
as a selfish shrinking from a scene, but as a mode of
self-discipline, as the thoughtful sympathy of a wise,
I would almost say an imaginative, certainly a kindly
man. This is Epicureanism in the best sense of the
word. Yet for all his intimacy (his intimacy goes
much further than this, and in his earlier satires to
embarrassing lengths)—for all that Horace is a
conscious artist, anxiously questioning the proper
form for this kind of self-expression: he decided
that the satirist was not a poet, and that his must
be almost the language of common life — *sermoni
propiora*. And therefore he banished from *Satura*
the felicitous art of the odes, and retained much
of the rough and casual versification of Lucilius,
especially in dialogue, the traditional part of *Satura*.
The object of Horace was simply to make the
metrical element in this form as unobtrusive as
possible. Lucilius perhaps half-consciously had the
same aim, and Persius in this naturally imitated
Horace. But the pioneers of classical satire in
England quaintly mistook the point. They thought
that the rough and informal verse was part of the
panoply of the satiric warrior, and like the Cynic's
shaggy beard and dirty shirt, a guarantee of the
highest motives.

[1] Sat. I. iv. 129.

As an artist Horace had to face two criticisms in his own day. Some said his satire was too severe. They could only have been those who had the best of reasons to dislike satire in any form. Others said that his verse lacked vigour. And that has been on the whole the feeling of later critics, certainly of later satirists. To the Elizabethans, as to Dryden, Horace's wit must have been faint and his salt insipid. They read into him some of their own factitious vehemence. And it was not till the Augustan age in England, when tact and common sense came by their own again, that the spirit of Horace found an echo. His influence tempered the venom of Pope; or perhaps it would be fairer to say that Horace's satire was a mould into which Pope could pour his kindlier feelings. But for all his miraculous ingenuity in adapting Horace to his own needs, Pope gives us something very different from Horace. He adds to him a vigour and a point that are Pope's.

Vigour and point were, indeed, after the work of the pioneers, the aim of the best of the English satirists, and that was why the master of later formal satire was not Horace or Persius, but Juvenal. For those are Juvenal's outstanding qualities. Whatever he may retain, from tradition or temper, of kindness or sympathy—and there is a great deal of this in Juvenal—the world has forgotten it, and remembers the invective and the epigram. Juvenal had no doubt a more sinful world to scourge than Horace, and was in some ways a better man. But the chief interest which Juvenal

provides in the history of satire is that he was a
disappointed man who happened to be a master of
rhetoric.   He belonged probably to a class, or at
least expressed the views of a class, to which there
is fortunately no modern parallel, literary men who
tried to supplement their small private means by
pressing their attentions on a body of supremely
indifferent patrons.   Such circumstances do not
encourage a rosy view of life, and Juvenal alone of
the Roman satirists seems to be a man with a real
personal grievance.   As a moralist he seems inferior
and less sincere, because less disinterested, than
Persius ; but he is in a far greater rage.   ' Juvenal's
spleen is raised and he raises mine,' said Dryden.
Then again the most elaborate system of rhetoric
which the world has ever known lay ready to
Juvenal's hand, and exactly fitted to his needs.
The lives of the poet tell us that he practised
declamation till middle age for pleasure, and then
took to writing satire.   But in truth his satire is still
declamation.   The satires on the Vanity of Human
Wishes and on the Women of fashionable Rome
follow in almost every detail the normal lines of the
rhetorical commonplace-books.   But Juvenal endows
them with a feverish life.

' Weigh Hannibal.   How many pounds does the
prince of generals scale ?   This is he whom once
Africa could not hold—the land washed by the
Moorish sea, stretching to the warm Nile and inland
to Aethiopia, and the home of the southern elephant.
He yokes Spain to his Empire ; he has leapt the
Pyrenees.   In his path Nature has set the snows of

the Alps.   He rives the rocks and melts mountains
with vinegar ; his foot is in Italy, yet on he hurries,
ever onward.   " 'Tis nothing done ", he cries, " till
we shatter their gates with our Punic soldiery, and
I plant my standard in Rome's midmost street."
Ah ! what a face was that, worthy of what a painter's
hand, where high on his African beast there rode
the one-eyed general !   And the end of him ?   Ah !
Fame, Fame !   Why, this same Hannibal must hurry
into exile and sit—a sight for men to wonder at—
a proud petitioner at a prince's court, till it shall
please his Bithynian sovereign to hold levée.   The
life that once embroiled a world is ended, not by the
sword, the rock, the javelin, but by that avenger of
Cannae, and of streams of blood—a ring.' [1]

By all the rules, the contrast between a heroic life
and a miserable death ought to lose by this elaborate
treatment.   But in fact it gains ; in every aspect but
the deepest, what I may call for brevity the poetic
aspect, it gains immensely.   But this is the finest
thing of its kind in Juvenal.   Elsewhere, and
especially in denunciation, he is not so happy.
When a consul's breach of an obsolete etiquette is
lashed with precisely the same energy as the grossest
vice, rhetoric dissolves in hysteria.

' Past the tombs of his fathers, fat Lateranus
dashes by in his fast curricle, and he, with his own
hands, yes he, a coachman consul, claps the brake on
the wheel.   It is at night : yes, but the moon sees it,
and the stars fix on him their wakeful eyes.' [2]

In passages like this the Elizabethan satirists found
only too much warrant for their pointless assumption

---

[1] Juvenal, *Satire* X, ll. 147-66.   [2] VIII, ll. 146 sqq.

of frantic rage. For all that Juvenal remains the prince of satirists. He is a master of irony, as Swift may remind us, the satirist's most effective weapon; and for whole satires he sometimes can keep alight a flame of articulate rage and scorn. He has a rich vocabulary of invective, but above all a turn for grim and penetrating epigram. This last is a gift which has found him most admirers. 'Juvenal is of a more vigorous and manly wit,' said Dryden; 'he gives me as much pleasure as I can bear.' It would be strange if a man with these qualities was not sometimes a poet. And there are a few passages in Juvenal which are genuine poetry. For one thing he can describe a scene as few Roman poets can, with short and trenchant strokes. Donne and Dryden, I think, seem to come nearest to him of the English satirists in this respect, but that is not because they imitate him : it is because they too have his terse and vivid pictorial imagination. Again, Juvenal, when he is off his satiric guard, surprises us by charming familiar poetry. He mellowed with age under good government. This is his vignette of himself and his friend taking a simple meal together, at his farm near Rome. They hear the roar of the circus through the clear Italian air. 'Let those boys watch it whose life it is to shout and make mad wagers, and sit by the side of a well-dressed girl. Let us off with our town clothes, while our wrinkled skin drinks in the spring sunlight. You may bathe before dinner even now without blushing, though it wants a whole hour to noon.' (For the Romans to dine early meant all the longer time for wine.) 'You could not do this five days running, for there's great boredom in a life like this too ; it's sparing enjoyment that makes our pleasures sweet.'[1]   And then there peers out from the extravagant hatred of the rich, what must have endeared Juvenal to Johnson, a genuine pity for the poor, a pity born of understanding and sympathy, perhaps of personal experience.   The best lines of unquestionable poetry which Juvenal ever wrote are wrung from him by the wrongs of the poor schoolmaster : 'The gods grant that the earth lie light and easy on our forefathers, and quicken fragrant crocuses and an eternal spring about their tombs, because they would that the master should be as sacred as the father to his boys.'[2]   But these things, though they belong to *Satura*, have taken me very far from satire.   It may be as well to summarize the positive effect on English satire, in its two most important periods, of the classical satirists taken as a whole : keeping in mind two facts, first, that the English satirists read the spirit of Juvenal in his angriest mood into all their classical models alike ; and secondly, that such a summary must give quite a false impression of many individuals, besides those even whom I except from it.

To the Elizabethans these models provided an inspiration for journalistic enterprise by suggesting general satire as a substitute for the lampoon and the controversy.   They guided and regulated the form and suggested the topics, the introductions, the conclusions.   And this was all to the good.   In satire the young author might win his spurs as he might in the sonnet or the pastoral.   Two of the

[1] XI, ll. 201 sqq.   [2] VII, ll. 207 sqq.

Elizabethans, however, stand outside this generaliza-
tion : Hall, because of his literary finish and comparatively wide interests; Donne, because of the
comparative sincerity of his hatred.   The satirist's
attitude is not a mere affectation in Donne, though
he makes the most of his natural stock and hugs
close his scorn of mankind.   When he says, ' Sir,
though—I thank God for it—I do hate perfectly all
this town,' he tells the mere truth, and in him alone
of his times does the hatred of a bore, a lawyer, and
a fool reach the altitude of a passion.   His satires
read like the reaction of nerves irritated beyond
endurance.   But even he can be seen sometimes
turning his jangled nerves to literary advantage for
the enjoyment of his private friends.

Much more Hall, who never convinces one of
genuine hate, who will sometimes transfer bodily,
and without change, a classical grievance to the
Tudor world.   But Hall has a wider field than
Donne, writes literary criticism in not too satiric
a spirit, and expresses his own personality—a much
more urbane and cultivated soul than his contemporaries'. He even anticipates sometimes the manner
of Pope, and polishes his couplet, and he has charming
passages of description.   His Arcadian Age, for instance :

Their royal plate was clay, or wood, or stone ;
The vulgar, save his hand, else he had none :
Their only cellar was the neighbour brook,
None did for better care, for better look.
Was then no plaining of the brewer's scape
No greedie vintner mixt the strainèd grape.

The king's pavilion was the grassy green,
Under safe shelter of the shadie treen.[1]

This is Donne's characteristic parallel passage :

Man's first blest state was naked; when by sin
He lost that, he was clothed but in beast's skin.[2]

The Elizabethan satirists tried to claim that their
satire was purely general; as a fact they contrived to
keep it lively by a good leaven of personal animosity
and partisan quarrel.   Yet on the whole classical
influence did make formal satire an artificial, hot-
house thing.   That is why it offers no resistance
to repressive edicts, and as a fashion dies down
quickly.   And during the period of the civil wars,
and for some time before and after them, classical
satire hardly appears—*inter arma satura silet*. Then
on a hint from France it appears again.   But France,
if I may borrow Drant's phrase, has pared its nails.
Whatever Boileau or Dryden, or even, after the
event, Pope may say of a desire to purge the passions, or to dissuade the dull and punish the wicked,
formal satire after the time of Oldham never seriously
attempted to do anything so ungentlemanly.   It was
absorbed in reproducing the gracefully malicious
conversation of the polite world.   Its weapons are
ingenuity and wit, and its doctrine is good sense.
But it was more malicious on the whole than grace-
ful.   For the ballads of the civil wars had left as
their legacy a tradition of violence directed against
the individual, and the rivalries of the newly founded
literary circles gave that spirit scope. So that Horace

---

[1] Book III, Satire I.   [2] *Satires*, I. 45.

and Juvenal still had their uses, and it became a
problem worthy of the *curiosa felicitas* of Pope to
find the precise place for Hervey and Lady Mary
Wortley Montagu among the victims of Horace.
Only by minute study of the parallel passages can
one come to a true estimate of Pope's ingenuity in
this kind of art. It is incredible. To speak of
classical influence on an art so deliberate and mature
is hardly possible. The Augustans wrote 'allusions'
to Horace for the same reason as Dryden wrote an
'allusion' to the Book of Samuel, because it was the
French fashion. But they wrote them as masters,
not as pupils. In his Third Satire Juvenal, speaking
of the Greek parasite, says 'in caelum miseris, ibit'
—'Tell him to go to heaven and he'll go.' Johnson's
version is a symbol of the freedom with which the
classics could be handled—'And bid him go to hell,
to hell he'll go.' In satire at any rate the Augustans'
treatment of the classics was a refutation of their
doctrine—'To follow nature is to follow them.' Nothing essential was added to English classical satire
after Johnson. With *English Bards and Scotch
Reviewers* it died, and over its tomb one may ask
what place it has occupied in art. As soon as it
is relieved from the pressure of immediate political
exigencies, satire assumes many forms. There is
that in which it puts off some of its own nature,
and happily blends with narrative and drama in the
sphere of the imagination. For a time it took this
form at Rome, but that early *Satura* had only an
incidental and occasional influence on English. In
our literature the satiric novels are the most striking

thing of the kind; among them are some of the
greatest works of English prose, and they are
untouched by the classics.

Where satire remains true to itself, if earnest and
disinterested, it might in the first place reform its
world, though only if, like earlier English satire, it
loved those whom it chastened.   But this aspect of
it is irrelevant to literature.   And in fact we find
that the satirist either simply hates, or far more often
simply pretends to hate.   When he honestly hates,
his work may have, I think, a double value.   It may
certainly have the incidental quality of wit.   But
it seems that it has a further and more essential
virtue.   This kind of satire expresses a passion in
the artistic way.   And the best examples of it avoid
the gravest danger by which satire is beset.   For
satire, dwelling on the meaner and grosser side of
life, may only tickle the palate of those whom it
would reform, and disgust those whom it would
encourage in virtue—unless it has vitality.   But
rage is at least alive, and there is a sublimity of
rage which, as Dryden felt, may heighten our own
vitality.   'Juvenal's spleen is raised, and he raises
mine.'   I should hesitate to call this poetry, but if
forced to do so, I should set it in the lowest rank of
poetry, since pure satire expresses the narrowest and
most one-sided view of life.   It is one of the infinite
riches of literature, but one of the least of them.
Donne and Johnson among English verse satirists
have most of this true satiric spirit; it was native
to them, but fostered by the kindred spirit of

Juvenal. Its fullest development is found not in verse satire at all, but in the prose of Swift.

Most satires do no more than pretend, if they even do pretend, to hate. And in these we look on at a game, not at a work of art. It is not nearly the best of the minor entertainments of literature. It is remarkable, for instance, how rarely the satirist can make you laugh. But such as they are, it was these that the classics influenced most and best. For the classics suggested to them just the qualities which have made them live, their lively pictures, their telling phrase, and their wit.

SENECAN TRAGEDY

By A. D. GODLEY

IT is not for us to dogmatize about the conditions which produce great literature. Some say with apparent probability that the chief condition is a great writer. Given that, which may be conceded even in a co-operative age, there are critics who say that your great writer may be produced under any conditions—democracy, despotism, or what not,—but that a literature born under despotism is as likely to be killed by democracy as a democracy-produced literature to be killed by despotism. But if we are to consider the relation of Roman despotism to Roman literature we may say with general truth that the production of really great works is not often found divorced wholly from the affairs of a nation, the practical business of life, affairs in the largest sense, individual needs and passions or national aspiration. Certainly the greatest Roman writers were always conscious of a practical purpose of some kind—always in touch with some aspect of national life. Remove that source of inspiration and Roman literature loses much if not all of its excellence. Lucretius is a teacher with a practical lesson for the world. The driving force behind Virgil is the consciousness that he is celebrating national life and

the greatness of Rome.   The *Thebaid* of Statius, for
all its occasional beauties, is for the most part a
frigid imitation of the least valued parts of the
Aeneid.   Under the early Empire and the rule of
an imperial bureaucracy the tendency was to limit
the relations of literature to the practical business
of life.   Politics were dangerous or uninteresting,
speech and action no longer free, interest in short in
contemporary thought and life necessarily hampered
—at least at Rome and in the vicinity of the
imperial court.   And that is what really matters,
for the provinces were not yet ripe for the development of a provincial literature.   Rome drew all talent
to herself and subjected it to Roman influences.
There, the poet of the Neronian age must have said
to himself what is said by an editor of Nonnus in
the troubled middle years of the nineteenth century
—' La mythologie nous reste, inoffensive et pour
ainsi dire innocente.'   That, to a Roman, meant
a great deal.   Mythology alone remained as a safe
subject—and Roman imagination, less vivid and less
poetical than Greek, had not the magic power that
could give life and immortality to the legends of
a remote antiquity.   There were many who attempted it, no doubt.   Juvenal, writing of course
much after Nero's reign and the lifetime of Seneca,
but speaking in the same satire of the danger of
topics drawn from contemporary life, gibes at the
eternal mythological poet.   No one — he says —
knows his own house better than I know all the
commonplaces of poetry—the cave of the winds, the
golden fleece, the fate of Hylas, and all the rest of

the stock-in-trade. One is entitled to assume that these mythological bards had not the seed of immortality in them. At least they have perished, and we only know their names by a reference here and there. Of all these triumphs of the recitation-hall the *Thebaid* alone survives,—and if survival be a test of superior merit the rest cannot have been great. What is the epic of the Silver Age which has really stood the test of time? It is the *Pharsalia*, the work of the one poet of a kind of opposition, the one who dared to give expression— if rhetorical rather than poetical—to a kind of regret for what had once been a political reality.

Probably then, at Rome, the literature which went for its inspiration to mythology was fore-doomed to mediocrity. But it also acquired under the combined influence of various circumstances a character of its own,—and a character which could not but damage dramatic literature. The Romans never had a serious drama ; and perhaps it was the fault of those who should have been the audience. Perhaps dramatist and spectator did not speak the same language : by the time of Nero I suppose that was so. Colloquial Latin was too different from literary. Perhaps again the Roman man in the street (who after all makes and unmakes drama) always preferred something at once agreeable and practical, like seeing men killed, or a bear-baiting. At any rate there were plenty of reasons why a mythological drama, going for its subjects to Greek legend, could never be really interesting to the general Roman public. Seneca's plays—*Hercules*

Furens, Troades, Phoenissae, Medea, Phaedra, Agamemnon, Oedipus, Thyestes, Hercules Oetaeus—are all mythological. And when I say Seneca, please assume that I mean Seneca the younger, the philosopher, the tutor of Nero. We will also assume that this Seneca is the author of the tragedies which are usually credited to him. (There is a controversy about this into which we need not enter ; for the present it seems probable that he wrote them, and those who take the Bacon side in the great Bacon-Shakespeare controversy may be comforted by the probability that a philosopher was also a tragic poet.) Plays of this kind, then, could not be acted with success : so that if you must write them, you wrote for 'private view' recitation, for the delectation of a literary coterie. Even poetry other than dramatic is apt to be very curiously affected by mutual admiration societies. We see that to-day. And drama which is not meant to be acted but to be read to your cultured friends, after the fashion of the day, is apt to become singularly undramatic. It is the consciousness of the stage that makes plays. Otherwise, uncorrected by the actual requirements of a theatre and an audience, the thing becomes a way of reproducing—and helping to form—the literary fashions of the age : it aims at the graces which appeal to the superior persons and the best literary culture of the day. Now the literary ideals of the Neronian period could be attained very well in drama,—provided always the drama was not meant to be acted. The Ciceronian and Augustan era— an age of great fluency, even verbosity, when

literature was not only luminous but also voluminous
—was succeeded by a reaction, as very often happens:
mostly because after a 'golden' age writing becomes
popular, and seeing that for one who can be great
there are about a thousand who can be clever,
the number of people who show off their cleverness
by trying to be in some way different from their
predecessors is very large. It was a mark of cleverness to be tired of the lengthy but plain and clear
development of the Ciceronian sentence, and to aim
at brevity and pithiness—even to obscurity. Further,
the more the educated public sees of literature the
more it criticizes language; and the things which
interest it are not always the deepest things: it
concerns itself with superficialities of style and form.
These matters please and attract: such a fine thing,
they say, to be able to dazzle with a curious new use
of an old word, or a display of erudition, and so on:
it is not so easy to judge the real $\mathring{\eta}\theta os$, but it is
comparatively easy to see what literary artifice is
likely to be most effective. People begin to play
tricks with words, and to use them less to bear
criticism as expressing a meaning than to be let off
as fireworks. This passion for effect, this continual
bid for applause, tends, in language, to preciosity
and the cult of the unusual. And as with language
so with treatment; and that is the more obvious of
the two in the Silver Age. In the *Dialogus* Tacitus
tells us that nobody now will stand the old, hum-
drum, tedious Ciceronian way of dealing with a case:
we must have something smarter and crisper than
that: 'laetitia et pulcritudo orationis,' 'poeticus

decor,' something that you can remember and quote,
a phrase, an epigram, a picturesque paradox. They
say of the Silver Age literature that it reads best in
quotations. There must at all hazards be something
to startle and arrest. It is continually trying to say
a thing in a new way. Juvenal and Statius are
always doing that. The literary tendency of the
day was formed and fostered partly by the requirements of recitation and the *assiduus lector*, partly by
the schools of rhetoric which taught you what to say
and how to say it—how to deal with a given topic
or situation, and which, in proportion as the art of
speaking was more and more divorced from the
actual business of life and became a drawing-room
accomplishment, taught exaggerated mannerisms
as a musician teaches a pupil to play the piano
effectively. Drama, according to the ideas of the
literary coterie, must be constructed by rule and
must have certain ingredients. There must be
declamatory passages to show your power of em-
phasizing a situation. There must be descriptive
passages to show off your erudition. There must
be pithy 'sententiae', epigrams, aphorisms, im-
pregnated perhaps with the current philosophy of
the cultured, to suit the taste for brevity and point.
Seneca the philosopher is the typical prose-writer
of the Silver Age: Quintilian the critic, who is
reactionary in the direction of a defunct Ciceronianism, considers Seneca's prose to be a danger to
literature. He says it has every fault that a prose
style can have. That is a matter of taste. What
is to the point is that Seneca the poet is also typical

of his age: in him we find that tendency to exaggerate, that lack of proportion, that straining after effect, which is the inevitable outcome of rhetorical schools. Seneca the tragedian is above all things a rhetorician. As he works on the lines of Greek tragedy, following in the main the plots laid down by Aeschylus, Sophocles, and Euripides, we find him always doing the same thing,—given a situation, trying to say the most brilliant, the most erudite, the most generally striking things about it.

As Euripides too is a rhetorician in his way, it is most natural to compare his method with Seneca's. He is certainly the least unlike Seneca of the three. He is very fond of setting out in long speeches all the arguments that can be used in a given situation. That is what Aristophanes blames him for,—that he makes his characters descend from the majesty and pomp of tragedy to argue like politicians or pleaders. They do that certainly ; but they do not forget their characters, and they are the more lifelike for their arguing ; it is the true rhetoric of persuasion : each states his case as plainly and persuasively as he can. An Euripidean speech is as plain and practical as a speech of Demosthenes or Lysias. It is just the argumentative method of real life ; whether the characters of tragedy ought to speak like that is another question. But Seneca's rhetoric is a very different thing from Euripides' eloquence. Somebody says of Juvenal—in a nobly mixed metaphor—that he ventriloquizes through a colourless puppet. Seneca does not do that exactly : his puppets are very highly coloured, stamped with the impress of

some one particular passion which has to be always
expressed; but puppets they are all the same, mere
mouthpieces for the clever arguments that would suit
with a given situation.   Seneca is very fond of stichomuthia—line-for-line dialogue : it is his usual way of
stating pros and cons.   It does not matter in the
least who is taking part in the Senecan *altercatio*—
whatever characters are on the stage, the dialogue
is a succession of thrust-and-parry repartees, each
speaker showing off his cleverness at parrying the
opponent's foil within the allotted space of a line, or
half a line, or even a quarter.   No matter who the
personages are, old or young, human or divine, slaves
or freemen, they all hurl epigrams at each other : very
often the stichomuthia is a succession of aphorisms
on life and conduct, for the most part Stoic aphorisms, as one would expect from Seneca.   It is the
rhetoric of *scores* rather than of serious argument.
Major premisses simply hurtle through the air like
shuttlecocks.   You hurl a general proposition at your
interlocutor : back comes *his* general proposition with
the inevitableness of a rebounding ball.   It is all very
brilliant and showy ; but the brilliance of electric
light leaves one rather cold.   What one looks for
in tragedy is character in action, not only brilliant
criticism of a situation, and Seneca's dialogue is so
deliberately clever in its pitting of argument against
argument that he diverts attention from everything
else (not to mention that he becomes very tedious in
the process) : one feels the too-cleverness-by-half
all the more when, as sometimes happens, the disputed
points in a stichomuthia are not really of primary

importance in reference to the main course of the play. But whether the dialogue be relevant or not, the audience is less likely to be purified by pity and terror when it is being continually challenged to admire a fencing-bout of brilliant wits.

A few passages selected almost at haphazard from the dialogue may serve to illustrate Seneca's manner. Here Medea and the Nurse are discussing the former's situation (*Med.* 160-73):

Nurse. Courage is good in season, then alone.
Medea. Courage hath every season for its own.
N. Thou hast no hope thy fortunes to repair.
M. Who feels no hope can never feel despair.
N. Betrayed by Jason and of friends bereft,
    What hast thou now of all thy greatness left?
M. Medea's left: in that tremendous name
    Is earth and sea and heaven's avenging flame!
N. Yet fear the King!
M.   My sire had been a king.
N. Dost not dread arms?
M.   Nay,—though from earth they spring.
N. Death here awaits thee.
M.   'Tis for death I'm fain.
N. Fly while thou may'st!
M.   Hath flight then brought me gain?
N. Medea—
M.   Ay, to that name I'll be true.
N. Think of thy children!
M.   And their father too.
N. Wilt thou not fly?
M.   Ay,—when I've wreaked my wrath.
N. Vengeance shall follow.
M.   I can bar its path.

When Clytemnestra contemplates killing Agamemnon, the plot obviously calls for stichomuthia.

Nurse. Thy fault is hidden if thou let it be.

Clytemnestra. This household's ill is plain for all
to see.

N. Is't not enough, the evil thou hast done?

C. Crime half-accomplished is for fools alone.

N. He who sins oft doth but his fears increase.

C. Yet fire and knife bring sickness oft surcease.

N. What should be last do not at first essay.

C. In straits like ours best is the headlong way.

N. Think of thy husband and thy marriage vows.

C. Ten years a widow, can I call him spouse!

Even Cassandra must play her part in this vein
(792-9):

Agamemnon. Here let us worship at this sacred
fane.

Cassandra. At such a temple was my father slain.

A. To Jove together let our prayers arise.

C. What? Jove who saved my house from enemies?

A. Thou art distraught: no Ilium meets thy view.

C. Ay, but it doth: Ilium and Priam too.

A. Take comfort, maiden: Troy thou dost not see.

C. Where Helen is there's Troy enough for me.

A. Thou'rt but a slave, nor shouldst thy mistress
fear.

C. A slave I am, but freedom's dawn is near.

A. Bid cease thy terrors, live with us in peace.

C. 'Tis death alone can bid my terrors cease.

A. Thee doth no danger in these halls await.

C. Perchance: for thee is danger dire and great.

A. What terrors then can threat a conqueror's
head?

C. The less he dreads the more he hath to dread.

It is a dead level of ready repartee. Whatever the
matter in hand and whoever the speaker, they have
always an epigram for the emergency. Medea,
despite the advice of Horace, ' Butchers her

mangled infants on the stage,' still pursuing them to
the end with the fatal *mot juste*; and one feels that it
is really better so, for had they lived for another page
they must certainly have prattled epigrams.

It is the weakness of a rhetorician like Seneca
that he over emphasizes everything for effect, non-
essential as well as essential. That is so with his
displays of erudition : one differentia of a good poet
is the way that he manages his learning. A great
poet like Virgil 'wears it lightly like a flower' and
makes it subserve his poetical purpose: a clever writer
like Seneca does not wear it lightly like a flower but
carries it like a porter carrying a trunk. Any character
of Seneca's may at any moment become oppressively
erudite in or out of season. It is as if they had
classical dictionaries in their pockets. No opportunity is lost for something effective and impressive
in this line. When Medea is to poison the bride
of Jason—which in Euripides' play she does very
simply, with no further particularization than φαρμάκοις
—all the poisons known to mythology are ranged
before us on the counter. This provides modern
scholars with a very convenient *locus classicus* on
the subject; but one cannot help feeling that poor
Creusa might have been settled quite comfortably
with a great deal less mythology; and the list of
drugs is so long and pompous that it delays the
action of the play and distracts the attention of the
reader. Similarly, in the Senecan version of the
Oedipus Tyrannus, Tiresias is not satisfied with
answering Oedipus, when consulted about the pestilence and its causes, out of his own head, as he

does in the Sophoclean version. In spite of the fact that he is anticipating the great scene of ἀνα-γνώρισις, and really making it unnecessary, he goes off to the underworld to consult the murdered Laius —who certainly had every right to know the truth of the business; and in order that he may find Laius it becomes necessary that all the most famous or infamous personages in Hades should be paraded, for no earthly or subterranean reason except to make a *mise en scène* for Laius and to show that Seneca knew his Lemprière. Similarly in *Hercules Furens* Theseus interrupts the action of the play with a highly ornamental passage on Hercules *aux Enfers*. These are episodes which overweight a play: of all tragedies, says Aristotle, αἱ ἐπεισοδιώδεις χείρισται: the result is something like 'Another Drury Lane Triumph', where spectacular realism distracts the attention of the spectator from the course of the play—if it has one. But that is Seneca's way. Evidently he writes not for representation but for recitation to an audience that wants 'purple patches', and he either has little sense of dramatic propriety or does not care to cultivate it. It is well enough that such a speech as Juno's at the opening of *Hercules Furens* should bristle with points. It is a very powerful statement of Juno's case against Jupiter. It is a Prologue and there is no hurry. But Seneca departs from the Greek treatment of great moments, where at any rate every reader must acknowledge the Greek method to be extremely admirable. He spoils the great scene of Oedipus' self-recognition by anticipating it.

In the play as written by Aeschylus all we know of
Agamemnon's death is the cry from within the palace,
coming at a moment when we are prepared for something terrible by the dark utterances of Cassandra.
For the moment, we guess the rest. That will not
do for Seneca. Here is a bloody murder, with a fine
opening for gruesome description. He does not indeed
kill Agamemnon on the stage : he is, I believe, careful
(rather surprisingly) to observe the convention of
only three actors, and a murder scene *plus* Cassandra
would necessitate four. So Cassandra stays outside the palace, but obliges with a description of
what she is privileged to see going on inside. No
detail is spared : Seneca is fond of gross physical
horrors : a cinematograph or a few sentences of Zola
could not do the thing more thoroughly. It is a fine
bit of description; but to declaim bloodcurdling
details at such a moment is essentially undramatic.
But nothing in Seneca's plays is really dramatic.
The schools of rhetoric taught, not how to present
character in action, which is the true business of
drama, but how to declaim upon a given situation.
A jealous wife in presence of her husband and her rival
—by what declamatory methods can she best show
her jealousy ? So, while in Sophocles' *Trachiniae*
Deianira is a particularly human and attractive
figure, partly jealous but much more compact of
love and gentleness, a very subtle presentation, in
Hercules Oetaeus she is a mere personification
of one particular passion : so, while Euripides tries
his hardest not to alienate our sympathies from
Phaedra—and does to a certain extent succeed—

in Seneca's play she is simply a personification of lust. She rants in this vein as Deianira rants jealousy. Each is a type of passion and talks accordingly. There is not a real human character in all the tragedies.

These dramas, then, are Roman in their dramatic weakness. But regard them not as dramas, but as vehicles for moral disquisition, which in part they are, and they are also Roman in their strength. For strength they undoubtedly have : it would be a grave injustice, and very ungrateful too, to toss them aside as mere unskilful copies of Greek tragedy. When the Romans took the trouble to speculate, what most interested them was morals. The greatest of the Silver Age writers are primarily moralists. Let Juvenal bewilder our judgement as he will with much rhetorical exaggeration, behind it all is a true *saeva indignatio* for outraged morality. Tacitus is far less interested in politics than in ethics. One need not speak of Seneca himself. Since the later days of the Republic the ethical aspect of Stoicism— that Stoicism which the sensible man Cicero found it easy to laugh at on occasion, but which the idealist Cato carried into practical life, to the embarrassment of politics—had appealed strongly to the Romans. Many were surprisingly captivated by that Stoic fantasy of an impossible virtue which could defy the slings and arrows of outrageous fortune : perhaps not so surprisingly either, for Nero and Domitian often deprived men of every other possession, and if a violent death must be faced the Stoicism which called death an actual good was the best way of making

terms with a painful situation.   Seneca's tragedies
are penetrated through and through with the philosophy of Seneca the prose-writer: that is, a philosophy Stoic in the main, yet eclectic, not refusing to
borrow from the Academics or even the Epicureans
occasionally.   However, it is Stoic on the whole;
and we may say broadly that all Seneca's characters
talk in the vein of the Porch.   Perhaps a captious
critic might find here another mark of want of veri-
similitude in the Senecan drama ; for how, he might
ask, could persons living by the light of pure reason,
and counting all external goods as nothing in comparison with virtue, have ever allowed their passions
to get their affairs into such a mess ?   That is perhaps
a frivolous question.   Seneca himself, who ranked
virtue above all things, was a millionaire, and Nero's
tutor.   However that be, Stoicism meets us on every
page: the Stoicism of Seneca the philosopher.   Virtue
is superior to all externals : tyranny and oppression
give it but more scope: 'imperia dura tolle, quid virtus
erit ?' says Megara in *Hercules Furens*.   'Virtutis
est domare quae cuncti pavent':

> Virtue thus
> Sets forth and magnifies herself: thus feeds
> A calm, a beautiful, and silent fire,
> From the encumbrances of mortal life,
> From error, disappointment—nay, from guilt.

To the Greek, the realist, death is an evil.   To
the Senecan characters death is nothing, even a
positive good: suicide is a luxury: just as under
the early Empire, we are told, the more reasonable

teachers of Stoicism found it necessary to warn their too ardent pupils that suicide might degenerate into mere selfish gratification of a desire. Even Polyxena, nay even the child Astyanax, dies like Cato, with an expressed conviction that death is an actual good. ' I would rather', says Oedipus in the *Phoenissae*, ' be forced to die than prevented from dying.'   No great dramatist has ever so contradicted the common voice of humanity. This contempt of death partly resembles that of the Christian martyr ; but the animating senti- ment is wholly different, and the Christian dies, after all, only to live.

Such a philosophy, expressed in a sententious and quotable manner—in what has been called ' a rolling fire of epigrams and concise and dazzling phrases ', is a potent antiseptic against oblivion.   Sir Walter Scott says : ' Tho' devoid of dramatic effect, of fancy, and of genius, the *Oedipus* of Seneca displays the masculine eloquence and high moral sentiments of its author : and if it does not interest us in the scene of fiction, it often compels us to turn our thoughts inward and study our own hearts.'   And much worse literature might have been kept alive through the Dark Ages by the great and famous name of Seneca. Anyhow, the nine tragedies did survive ; and at the period of the revival of learning we find them familiar and famous, far more so than in the twentieth cen- tury.   Seneca was translated : he was acted in the University of Cambridge : Skelton gives ' Senek with his tragedies' a place among famous classical writers : Ascham, while entertaining the paradoxical idea that Greek tragedies are as good or better,

talks of 'our Seneca'. These and more instances
are to be found in modern books, and one need not
labour the point. The general statement is true—
that no classical writer is so important in the history
of the modern drama. Seneca suffers much from
being necessarily compared with the great dramas
between which he forms a link : let him at least get
credit for being that link. Every nascent drama
must have models, or, at any rate, catches eagerly at
whatever will serve for a model, and Seneca was
ready to hand for the service of the earliest English
writers for the stage. He was in fact the only
accessible model : Greek study was as yet in its
cradle. Indeed, had Englishmen been able to draw
directly from Greek sources, would they have done
so in preference to copying from the Latin version ?
Every nation gets the drama which is best suited to
it. Is the magnificent restraint of Aeschylus, Sophocles, and Euripides really popular even now ? Does
such a representation as Reinhardt's and Harvey's
(and of course Sophocles') *Oedipus Tyrannus* go to
prove that ? I hardly think it. At any rate it
appears that the 'Hellenic spirit' has as a matter of
fact never contributed much to the making of tragedy
in England. Average English audiences—and the
Elizabethan dramatists always had in their mind the
necessities of the actual stage and the tastes of the
actual audience—have to be 'purified by means of
pity and terror' in other and less subtle methods.
Moral edification is dear to the heart of the British
public, and violent and bloody actions are still
dearer. 'Ne pueros coram populo' was all very well

for the Theatre of Dionysus, but it will never do for
Covent Garden. Seneca provided moral reflections
and also physical horrors ; in these respects, as the
early English dramatists saw very well, he was the
master whom they had to imitate ; while they had
nothing to learn from him as playwrights, they were
quite able to take the details and properties which
suited their purpose. How far they went in actual
imitation it is not very profitable or interesting to
inquire. A Senecan convention was in the air, no
doubt. He gave the framework of tragedy, five
acts, the chorus,—and it is said with probability that
certain stock characters may come from him, the
conventional tyrant, the Nurse, the Ghost. But it
cannot be said that all who follow the Senecan model
had therefore gone straight to him as to the fountain-
head. The ideas or methods of treatment were in
the air. Here and there a dramatist has obviously
read the Senecan plays. Marston is the clearest case
among the Elizabethans. Jonson (he of the ' learned
sock ') again leaves us no room for doubt. In
Catiline and *Sejanus* there are passages which are
verbatim renderings of *Hercules Furens*. Jonson is
penetrated by the Senecan $\mathring{\eta}\theta o s$. And of course it
would be easy to make out on the face of it that
Shakespeare might have gone to the same source.
Richard III is a typical unredeemed tyrant, always
speaking and acting tyrannically, a very Senecan
character : he is something like Lycus in *Hercules
Furens*. Many ideas are common to both. But
there is nothing in that, really. They are the great
and obvious ideas of humanity, the immortal truisms

which must be present in all high tragedy: 'what
oft was thought but ne'er so well expressed.' Compare *Macbeth*, v. iii :

> I have lived long enough : my way of life
> Is fallen into the sere, the yellow leaf :
> And that which should accompany old age,
> As honour, love, obedience, troops of friends,
> I must not look to have,

with *Hercules Furens*, 1258–62 :

> cur animam in ista luce detineam amplius
> morerque nihil est : cuncta iam amisi bona,
> mentem arma famam coniugem gnatos manus,
> etiam furorem.

There is a kind of similarity, no doubt; but to allege
a debt would be nearly as irrational as to say that
one arithmetician has borrowed from another because
both concur in saying that two and two make four.
At any rate, if you want to admire Seneca, it is best
not to study him in juxtaposition to Shakespeare and
Marlowe. If they do borrow, they do so as poets ;
and turn second-rate into high poetry.

Latin rhetoric could never continue to influence
the English stage, except sporadically. French aims
at similar rhetorical finish ; hence the enduring influence of Seneca on the French drama. His manner
of expression is congenial to Corneille and Racine,
even to Victor Hugo and perhaps even Rostand :
rhetorical purple patches and rhetorical rotundity of
phrasing appeal to France as they never could to
England. In fact, we very soon outgrew the
influence of Latin tragedy—'the main stream of

English tragedy flowed in different channels.' It must be said we also outgrew the habit of having a drama. So that the Senecan style on the evidence may be called a preservative of tragedy. Perhaps the recent revival of 'serious' plays on the stage may disprove that. For there is nothing of the Senecan tradition in Mr. Galsworthy; and we look for it in vain in the plays of Mr. Bernard Shaw.

INDEX